Tools for you, the dreamer

Dreams give you information about yourself that you cannot obtain anywhere else. Listening to your dreams involves allowing your inner voice to speak to you. Sometimes you will find that the symbols have the same meaning for everyone. At other times the symbols will have meanings unique to you. This interactive system for dream interpretation will help you determine the personal messages of your dreams to suit your individual situation. The book and software will guide you in the right direction, with suggestions and questions to facilitate your exploration of the mysterious communications from your unconscious.

Learn to identify and interpret the many different kinds of dreams:

Prophetic dreams

Recurrent dreams

Animal dreams

Erotic dreams

Children's dreams

Epic dreams

Physical dreams

Dreams of the personal daimon

Lucid dreams

Confirmation dreams

Astral dreams

Waking dreams and visions

Nightmares

The more of yourself you bring to your dream work, the greater the eventual reward. The content of your dreams is at least as vast as your waking life. It provides a new frontier of personal exploration—an interior world only you can investigate. You now have the tools to track and record your journey into the dream realm.

About the Author

Dr. Stephanie Clement has an M.A. in humanistic psychology and a Ph.D. in transpersonal psychology. She is also a certified hypnotherapist and has been a professional astrologer for twenty-five years. Clement has used dream work as a therapeutic tool for nearly twenty years. She has lectured and given workshops in the United States and Canada on psychological counseling and astrology. Clement's published books include *Charting Your Career: The Horoscope Reveals Your Life Purpose; Decanates and Dwads; Counseling Techniques in Astrology;* and *Planets and Planet-Centered Astrology.* In addition, she has published numerous articles on astrological counseling, charts of events, and counseling techniques.

About the Software Designer

Terry Lee Rosen has a degree in criminal justice and is doing graduate work in business. He teaches computer programming at Front Range College in Colorado and is an avid gamer, artist, and student of tarot and other metaphysical subjects. Rosen's strong interest in creative writing drew him into the production of the dream journal program.

To Write to the Author and Software Designer

If you wish to contact the author or software designer or would like more information about this book, please write to the author or designer in care of Llewellyn Worldwide and we will forward your request. The author, designer, and publisher appreciate hearing from you and learning of your enjoyment of this book and how it has helped you. Llewellyn Worldwide cannot guarantee that every letter written to the author or designer can be answered, but all will be forwarded. Please write to:

Stephanie Clement and Terry Lee Rosen
℅ Llewellyn Worldwide
P.O. Box 64383, Dept. K145-7
St. Paul, MN 55164-0383, U.S.A.
Please enclose a self-addressed stamped envelope for reply,
or $1.00 to cover costs. If outside U.S.A., enclose
international postal reply coupon.

Many of Llewellyn's authors have websites with additional information and resources. For more information, please visit our website at http://www.llewellyn.com.

Dreams

WORKING INTERACTIVE

STEPHANIE CLEMENT, PH.D.
SOFTWARE DESIGN BY TERRY LEE ROSEN

2001
Llewellyn Publications
St. Paul, Minnesota 55164-0383, U.S.A.

First Edition
Second Printing, 2001

Book design and editing by Joanna Willis
Cover design by Anne Marie Garrison
Software design by Terry Lee Rosen

Library of Congress Cataloging-in-Publication Data
Clement, Stephanie Jean.
   Dreams: working interactive / Stephanie Clement; software design by Terry Lee Rosen.—
1st ed.
     p. cm.
  Includes bibliographical references.
  ISBN 1-56718-145-7
   1. Dreams. 2. Dream interpretation. I. Title.

BF1078 .C54 2000
154.6'3—dc21

00-034805

Llewellyn Publications
A Division of Llewellyn Worldwide, Ltd.
P.O. Box 64383, Dept. K145-7
St. Paul, MN 55164-0383, U.S.A.
www.llewellyn.com

 Printed in the United States of America on recycled paper

Other Books by Stephanie Clement

What Astrology Can Do for You
(Llewellyn, 2000)

Charting Your Career: The Horoscope Reveals Your Life Purpose
(Llewellyn, 1999)

Counseling Techniques in Astrology
(American Federation of Astrologers, 1992)

Planets and Planet-Centered Astrology
(American Federation of Astrologers, 1992)

Decanates and Dwads
(American Federation of Astrologers, 1983)

This book is dedicated to three groups of people:

First, to the families of the authors,
without whom studies and personal development
would never have been undertaken;

Second, to the numerous clients and friends
who contributed their dreams and visions
in therapy, conversation, and correspondence;

Third, to the numberless individuals
who developed the computer and its programming,
making this interactive book and the dream journaling program possible.

Contents

Preface

Individuation

Carl Jung developed his theory of individuation as the result of long series of dream interpretations with his clients. In the context of such series, psychic movement in some particular direction can be observed. If there are houses in the dreams, the nature of the houses changes. If there are animals, the dreamer's relationship to them changes. Individuation is the seemingly planned and relatively orderly process of development within the individual.

In his work called *Dreams,* Jung stated: "The question whether a long series of dreams recorded outside the analytical procedure would likewise reveal a development aiming at individuation is one that cannot be answered at present for lack of necessary material." He hypothesized that analysis speeds the developmental process (1974, 76).

Much of Jung's writing concerning dreams was done in the first decade of the twentieth century. Since that time many volumes of dream research have been compiled. We have more information about dreams now and may find that with or without a therapist, dreams form a picture of our developmental processes. Neither the analysis nor recording of dreams is essential for the evolution of consciousness. Rather, they aid dream reconstruction and interpretation in the same unexpected way a diary aids biography. I believe that intense psychological work is not necessary for everyone. In some cases the therapist can act as a guide through difficult territory when dream content is incomprehensible and disturbing. However, for most of us the dream process works well, and we may want to consider the "if it ain't broke, don't fix it" approach to individuation.

I strongly believe that dreams provide all of us with information about ourselves that we cannot obtain in any other way. Listening to your dreams involves allowing your inner voice to speak to you. This is radically different from listening to outside voices. For one thing, no one else can hear your inner voice clearly. Secondly, each person has a personal understanding of the ordinary events of the world and of the collective mind. Your understanding of the collective comes through your own unconscious, and therefore comes through the most personal filter possible. What you have in common with others' dreams is the nature of archetypal symbols—symbols that emerge in all cultures and carry a shared meaning. What you do not have in common is the personal meaning of these symbols and their degree of importance. A symbol that frightens one person can be erotic to another. Symbols can be archetypes or they can represent other symbols. A fox can be clever, it can be a thief, a pretty lady, or it may mask the color red. Or a fox may simply be a fox.

Symbols are transient. What has religious significance, such as a cross, may the next day become a mundane mark as you cross something off a list. Symbols may be containers, like a heart-shaped locket which conceals the more specific symbol of a loved one. Or they may be the seed of another symbol's fruit—a dream of money that purchases a house. Is the house then a symbol of finding a home, or a prison? The more rigid your interpretations of symbols, the more surprising or elusive they will become, for they always arrive with a feeling, always deepen with context, and always refuse a formula. No equation, no matter how complex, can ever encompass the life of dreams. Often, just as we are applying the most careful scrutiny to details, sometimes even as we dream, the point explodes with sudden obviousness—a cream pie in the face.

Always respect the possibility that there is or will be another context for your dream symbols in time or memory, some heretofore unconsidered connection in dreaming. The fox may be a trickster, the face of consciousness' fathomless capacity to universalize, reminding us that there is no treasure as limitless as the mirror of knowledge that may evoke the image of anything to recall the meaning of everything.

Part I

The Variety of Dreams

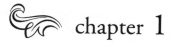 chapter 1

Dream Analysis

The analysis of dreams is nearly as old as the world. In all cultures records of dreams and their meaning can be found, and in some cultures dreams are considered as important as waking reality, if not more so. Each culture provides a rich context in which its people's dreams can be interpreted. In addition, each culture provides a rich resource of archetypal symbols that cross cultural lines to invade people's dreams in other societies. Carl Jung studied symbols wherever he could find them and organized them into a universal system. He believed that these symbols were the contents of the collective unconscious, and that individuals tap into these contents through dreams and other mechanisms. He postulated that dream contents, no matter how foreign to the waking mind, have personal and also transpersonal meaning—that is, they reflect all human experience contained in the collective mind—and are accessible to each of us through dreams and visions.

Study of the psychology of different social and cultural groups reveals that dreams hold significance across a broad range of peoples. Study of actual dreams reveals both the diversity of individual dream experiences and the wealth of interpretive possibilities within and across cultures. This book is intended to introduce the richness of possible interpretations and to present a systematic approach to dream analysis. Your personal dreams will very likely take you in a particular direction, using some, but not all, of the techniques presented here. The purpose of this book is to help you discover your own dreaming style, identify the different types of dreams you regularly experience, and help you discern the messages found in your dreams.

Symbols are objective, visible representations of something less visible, less concrete, but generally agreed upon by people within a culture and sometimes throughout all cultures. Every symbol in your dreams has a conscious component—you recognize what it is—and an unconscious component—you don't know what it means, or you don't know why it is in the dream, but you know it is important.

Some symbols are conventional, agreed-upon signals for the conscious mind. An example is a diamond-shaped road sign with a picture of a person or deer on it. The picture is an indication that you should watch out for a person or deer. A curvy line with an arrow at the upper end indicates the shape of the road ahead. Another example is the use of Greek letters to represent mathematical functions.

Some symbols are personal. They have an outer objective meaning, but the inner personal meaning may be quite different. For example, when animals are being trained, they come to associate colors or shapes with specific rewards. Other animals will not have the same associations. We are trained in a similar way. The smell of my mother's favorite perfume symbolizes "mother" to me, but it probably would not for someone else.

What I am calling symbols in this book are things that have much broader, even universal meanings. The circle and its center form a universal symbol for both the sun and for wholeness. The circle and its quarters are universally understood to indicate a center and the directions of the compass on the conscious level, while it refers to four fundamental approaches to the world (thinking, feeling, sensation, and intuition) on a less conscious level.

When you are considering a dream, you are the only person who can determine which dream objects and events are symbolic and which are simply included to ensure continuity of the dream story. If my brother is in a dream that is actually about him, I can consider him as a symbol, but he really is my brother, after all. It may be more interesting to examine what he is wearing, how he sounds when he speaks, or other features of his presence in the dream.

If you are a mathematician, the symbols of your craft are just that; they are not likely to have other, deeper symbolic meanings as they might for someone else. Context is very important when you are considering symbols. The dictionary provided in this book and on the accompanying CD-ROM supplies food for thought about each symbol. I hope you are encouraged to consider each dream symbol from your personal point of view as well as from the perspective I have provided. The two approaches may have both common ground and significant divergence.

The Complex

As you examine a series of dreams, you will begin to see patterns. Often dreams reveal complexes (organizational factors) within the unconscious. A complex is like a web of associations within the unconscious mind, and is outside the control of the conscious mind. A complex has both its disturbing and supportive aspects. On the less constructive side, we have associations that may once have been meaningful and helpful, but that are now serving only to retard further development. For example, if your only association with a stove is that it will hurt you, you may have trouble preparing meals because of the associated fear of injury. On the creative side, complexes offer associations that enrich your life—they offer alternative meanings for you to consider. The oven may be associated with pregnancy, for example, as might any container. To the extent that a complex is harmful, it needs to be analyzed and understood in order to reduce its limiting effect. To the extent that a complex is helpful, it also needs analysis and understanding in order to garner its greater value.

A series of dreams that repeat certain symbols can serve to illuminate an area of your unconscious mind. Approach the center of a complex, large or small, by examining the repetitive elements and considering their subtle variations. But remember, the goal is not to pound the complex out of existence. There are at least two ways to gain valuable results from listening to your dreams where complexes are concerned:

1. Reduce the mythological quality in order to make the information conscious and therefore useful. You may want to examine and understand symbols, however disturbing they may be initially, in order to reduce their painful symptoms. Your examination of dream symbols helps to bring your hidden impulses under conscious control.

2. Preserve the mythological character in order to retain the "spice" of life. The rich field of your dreams shows, first and foremost, the richness of your mind. As you examine unfriendly dream content, you may find that your dreams gradually change to become more supportive of your waking life. It's more fun to think of your dreams as personal Hollywood-style productions, produced and directed by your sleeping self in collaboration with your waking personality.

Each kind of dream has its own character and its own potential purpose. Some dreams are designed to cut through powerful complexes in order to bring you the information you need. Dream journaling (see below) provides you with a consistent approach to understanding this inner source of personal wisdom.

The Variety of Dreams

Everyone dreams every night. Dreaming is an activity that is almost as familiar as eating or walking, yet our dreams often mystify us. The juxtaposition of persons known to us, places and experiences separated by great time and distance, and sometimes stark symbols can make a dream into a kind of fiction that defies logic. Yet the dream is yours and no one else's. And therefore it is your dream to interpret. No dictionary can decide what the symbols mean. The dictionary only provides suggestions of general meanings. You have to decide what the symbols mean for you in the context of the dream and your life at the time you have the dream.

The following chapters examine different kinds of dreams and provide information about how to record, examine, and understand them. As you begin to work with your own dreams, you will find that they will speak more clearly, providing a rich resource of information and feelings. They will help you organize your life, make decisions, and take action. They become strong allies who accompany you along your personal path of spiritual development.

As you read about the different kinds of dreams, you may find that some of your dreams don't fit easily into one category. You may feel that a dream fits in more than one of the definitions. When this happens you can keep an open mind and wait for another dream or the natural course of events to reveal its specific meaning. You may decide that one dream serves two or more purposes. Just like you work out a complex problem in your daily life, a dream deals with complexities in its own way.

Dream Journaling

I have found it is helpful to have a consistent approach to dreams. Perhaps my dream mind also found it helpful, because the more I worked with my dreams in a specific way, the more information I seemed to get. I feel that the waking ego, the dreaming ego, and the unconscious mind learn to work together to provide images and information that can be understood, and that this work leads to a more satisfying life.

Dream working involves using your dreams for some practical outcome. In psychoanalysis, dreams are used to explore the unconscious regions of the mind. The intention is to discover the causes of mental distress or illness and resolve them. In analytical psychology, the unconscious realm is thought to include far more than just the source of an illness. Dreams include mythological references that connect us to larger, even universal values. The mythic dream could also be the source of information about the meaning of your own life.

In cultures around the world, dreams are shared with others as part of daily life, and the dreams' meanings may have a broad social impact. Literature is filled with examples of dreams. For example, Caesar's wife, Calpurnia, dreamed of notable Roman citizens washing their hands in blood that flowed from Caesar's statue. She took this as an omen, yet Caesar did not heed her warning.

Psychoanalysis and many other methods of dream work include interaction with other people. You will find that you can keep a completely private dream journal using the CD-ROM accompanying this book and derive personal benefit from it. You may also find that sharing your dreams enriches the experience.

This chapter outlines one approach to working with your dreams. It will serve to examine the contents of dreams, provide a structure for organizing their images and characters, and evoke their meaning. The dream tutorial on the enclosed CD-ROM lists a number of questions. Use it to prompt your memory for the details of your dream. You will probably find that you don't need this form after a while, but it may be very useful for expanding your understanding of dreams when you start the journaling process.

A. Recording the dream

It is important to record the dream exactly as it occurred, to the extent that this is possible. Because dream details fade over the minutes or hours after awakening, it is essential to record the dream immediately.

You may find that you remember more than one dream, so you can either record any that you remember, or the one that stands out as the most significant.

Record the dream without any editorial comments. Become a trained observer of your own dreams. Don't analyze them as you write, or edit out inconvenient content. By the same token, don't obsess about every tiny detail of pattern and color. Simply record the places, character, and events.

A "just the facts" approach will insure a good beginning. Later you may find yourself imitating the narrative styles of particular dreams. A storyteller does not always record his tale in the first person, nor is a fairy tale told the same way as a detective story. Not that you need to consciously parody William Faulkner at 3:00 A.M. Rather, allow the spirit of the dream to imbue your words when it will. Stream of consciousness is, after all, not just a name for a writing style, it is the narration of dreams. I find it helpful to tell all dreams as though they are happening in the present, since in this way I seem to re-enter the dream and remember more.

After you have recorded the dream, begin to examine its contents. The intention is not to judge or edit, but rather to consider them in an open-minded fashion.

B. Main characters

First consider the persons known to you. Record how you know the people. You may want to note whether these people were acting like themselves in the dream, of if they seemed to be out of character. Then consider dream characters not previously known to you.

C. Main features of the dream

Your dream is like a drama. The stage setting and historical period influence the way the action unfolds and offer insight into the deeper meaning of the dream. Throughout the dream you may identify buildings, costumes, peculiar speech, or other factors that tell you when and where the dream takes place.

You may also want to consider the time of day in the dream. Some black-and-white dreams may at first seem to take place at night because they are dark but may really be occurring in the daytime.

D. Action, scene, and characters

Which of these dream elements dominate the dream? For instance, if you were lost in a castle, the scene is paramount, whereas if you have a conversation with someone, character is more important, or if you are in a battle, action is key. You may have already recorded these items, but a list is sometimes helpful when you examine the dream. You may be able to make connections that were not obvious in the narrative.

E. Symbols in the dream

Note the symbol and its usual associations. When you record the dream in the CD-ROM's program, words will be highlighted and you can read their entries in the dream dictionary. Then you can choose whether or not to incorporate that entry into the dream document itself. You will also be able to add your own symbol entries and definitions that are not already in the dictionary.

Ask yourself if the symbol is familiar to you (e.g., is the tree in your dream a particular tree you have seen?). If it is not familiar, note your feelings and why it is symbolic in the context of the dream.

F. Personal and archetypal significance

Everything in a dream has some personal significance. Otherwise it would not be in the dream at all. You may not grasp the significance immediately, but later you may see how an odd item fits into the larger picture of your dream life.

Some dream contents also have the same meaning for people in different cultures and historical periods. These archetypal dream elements connect you to a larger collective mind. Carl Jung stated that some dream elements "have never been in consciousness and so could not be the result of repression, which is a personal matter. They are impersonal, or collective" (Bennet 1967, 65). Jung expanded on Freud's concept that memories are repressed in the unconscious to include memories that have never been conscious, but that are part of a larger, mythic, cultural consciousness. When you dream on this archetypal level, you may at first find the dream content fantastic, but later you may come to understand how your dream life reflects or incorporates information that is shared cross-culturally.

In thinking about the content of your dream, consider the following: (a) How does the dream connect to your personal circumstances? Certain symbols have both personal impact and archetypal significance. For example, if you have a pet tarantula, spiders may be fairly commonplace to you; yet, they also symbolize centering and the weaving of fate throughout our lives. (b) What is the larger social, spiritual, and/or transpersonal context of the dream? Even ordinary dream scenes often include messages and meaningful details that help you make important social or spiritual decisions. For example, a dream figure's clothing that seemingly has nothing to do with the content of the dream may suggest a change in your path.

G. Type of dream

Using the models in the following chapters, identify the type or types of dream your dream seems to fit. Consider how the types are appropriate to your present circumstances. Is the dream in which you're standing beneath a waterfall symbolic of your past life washing away, or is it a clue that the roof over your bedroom is leaking?

H. My feelings during the dream and when I awoke

Sometimes you feel a certain emotion during a dream, while at other times you seem to be observing, rather like watching a movie. Some dreams evoke little or no feeling within the dream, but you feel strong emotions upon awaking. Sometimes you don't remember the dream, but you awake with strong emotions. These variations can be significant, as they indicate the relative intensity of the dream message and the intensity of its impact on your conscious mind. What is the outcome of the dream? Does your dream self get what it wants or needs? Is the dream incomplete or pointless? Does it even have an ending?

I. Later thoughts or feelings

Later on you may develop an insight about the dream or your feelings may change. The act of considering the dream content can surely change your attitude toward its contents. Great fear in a dream, for example, may cause you to consider some factor in your waking life that otherwise might have been ignored.

The Ritual Process of Dream Work

Dream working is serious business. Through dream work you attempt to develop a friendly relationship with your less conscious being. Therefore, a more formal approach can establish the seriousness of your conscious intention. Dream work also evokes a safe context in which to examine your own beliefs and feelings. Thus, considering the process as a ritual can be beneficial. The following steps outlining the ritual process are taken from *Mandala* by Jose Argüelles and Miriam Argüelles and have been adapted for the dream working process.

1. Many people find that providing the proper writing materials is one way to demonstrate respect for the process. This corresponds to some extent with the process of purifying the ground on which a ritual can work. Using a journal only for dreams shows an interest that cannot be conveyed by writing on the back of grocery receipts and leaving them scattered about. Thus the cover of the journal can be symbolic—a picture of a spirit animal or landscape. The color of your pen and its ink can be evocative, as can the texture and color of the paper. You may wish to have room to make sketches that characterize particular dreams, adding a visual meditation to the process, which may then stimulate a pictorial dialogue within future dreams.

2. Centering yourself is accomplished by staying in the dream feeling as you begin to write. This is most easily accomplished if you record the dream immediately upon awakening. Otherwise it is easy to lose the feeling of the dream. You can cultivate a kind of split consciousness by remaining relaxed, teaching yourself to wake up the aspect of yourself that writes, while allowing part of your mind to remain in a kind of reverie, extending the dream state in the same way you can drive a car and have a conversation at the same time.

3. Orientation consists of stating the scene as the dream opens, and then recording changes of scene as they occur.

4. You won't be constructing the dream, but you will be recording it just as it occurred. The plot and characters of the dream, symbols and actions, are all part of the record of the dream. Keep in mind that sequence is not always important. Dreams cut and splice time and place like a mad movie director, seemingly to confound our hyper-logical tendency to understand everything in a predetermined order. Thus, if there is something at the end of the dream that

you feel is urgent, by all means write it down immediately and let the rest of the dream catch up to it, since the rest may only have been obligatory material to set up a punch line that explains everything in and of itself. Don't worry if you remember details of the first part when you are writing about a later scene. You can make notes in the margin or add the details later. Also, you can do this kind of rearranging when you enter the dream into the program.

5. Examine and analyze the dream, and even meditate on its form and contents. This involves looking at everything in the dream and considering how you think and feel about each detail. You may wish to discover other means of recording your dreams, such as making drawings, sculptures, dances, or integrating them into whatever creative work you pursue. Telling someone else your dreams (someone trusted and patient who preferably does the same with you) is helpful. Verbalization and feedback often reveal new insights. You can use your dictaphone or tape recorder and read the dream into an auditory record.

6. You can close the process of recording dreams clearly and precisely. You need to get into the activities of the day and leave the dream state. I find that setting the journal aside and putting on slippers and a robe accomplish this. I am wrapping myself in the fabric of my waking life and leaving the bed coverings that accompanied me in the dream state.

7. As you gather your thoughts for the coming day, you can acknowledge the dream and its message. You have opened the door to deeper personal understanding of yourself and your dream process, and you can let the dream contents simmer on their own. An occasional dream will not be set aside so easily. While most dreams fade within minutes when you awake, some stay with you vividly, even for years. Notice if this happens.

8. You now have the opportunity to take any new insights you have gained and incorporate them into your daily activities and into your world view.

Most likely you will find that after a few days you will incorporate these ritual steps into your dream work without giving them much thought. In fact, you will probably begin to see the ritual form being acted out in a number of ways in your daily life. Or you may begin to notice, despite their chaotic surfaces, that your dreams themselves reflect ritual structures. Most human activity involves some ritual behavior, and you will probably become more aware of it as you work with dreams.

If you are familiar with symbol systems like astrology or tarot, you may find that your dreams frequently incorporate these symbols. The symbols themselves may broaden to include ordinary details of your surroundings. In this way dream analysis helps to identify the meaningful relationships among the elements of your life. Synchronicity is the arising of meaningful relationships without any discernable cause. In other words, your dream of a brown dog does not cause a brown dog to cross your path. Yet that dog may remind you of the dream and help you see its deeper meaning.

You may also find that you are comfortable with an astrological or other ritual structure and prefer to use that as a basis for approaching your dreams. Dreams tend to fit into general categories or sets. You may find that yours fit into an allegorical format that reflects your studies or reading.

Prayer for insight can also be a part of the process. When I am struggling with a problem, I think of it as I go to sleep and ask for a dream to help me find a solution. When I have dreams, I try to consider whether they can be helpful in resolving questions in my waking life. Whether you believe your dream messengers are spirit guides, angels, or simply your dreaming ego, they don't have to appear in a dream to be behind the message you receive.

Expanding Your Dream Awareness
Using the CD-ROM Program

Once you finish recording your dream and you use the program to analyze it, you may find that certain symbols are not included in the dictionary exactly as you have written them. You can look up similar words in the book (e.g., try "goddess" for "Durga"). What you find may be more general yet still helpful. Any word that you type into the dream field will be compared to the program's dictionary entries.

Suppose your dream symbols are not in the program's dictionary at all. You can create a personal entry by researching them in books, on the Internet, or in other sources, or you can simply record in the dictionary your impressions, perhaps with a date. Then if the symbols come up again in later dreams, you can easily connect to the previous dream. One advantage of the personal dictionary is that you can identify dream elements that have powerful importance for you, even if they are not universal symbols.

Another interesting way to track symbols is to record waking experiences that tie into your dreams. For example, if you have a problem you are wrestling with at work, you can write about it in the journal and see what associations arise through the analysis. Also, if you experience synchronicity between dreams and waking experience, or if you experience déjà vu, you can record that. By doing so, you honor your personal relationship to the world around you, to the inner worlds of your mind, and to the infinite.

Perhaps you will think of additional ways to use the program. Please consider writing to Llewellyn Worldwide, the publisher, at the address in the front of the book. Your ideas may be added to the next version of the program or the next edition of the book. Also be sure to send in the registration information so Llewellyn can make you aware of updates to the program and the dictionary.

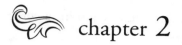 chapter 2

The Initial Dream

The Strafing Mission

I am a child—about four or five years old. I am sitting on the side of a hill on a sunny day. There are flowers around me, mostly yellow. The sky is blue. There are other hills across a small valley. As I am sitting, I hear a buzzing sound, and then see what appear to me to be German bombers flying over the hill, crossing my field of vision from left to right. They swoop down close to the ground in the valley and drop fat black bombs. The bombs hit the ground, but all that happens is that there are puffs of yellow smoke, reminding me of stink bombs. I can smell the sulfur.

The first dream you consider as you read this book can be taken as the initial dream. If you begin psychotherapy, the first dream you tell the therapist about will be considered the initial dream. If you begin a new job, move to a new place, or undertake any major life change, the first dream you recall after the change becomes the initial dream for the new venture. As with any dream, the content of your initial dream is your own personal content, and must be interpreted by you to suit *your* situation. Other people can offer suggestions, or their own interpretations, but ultimately you find the personal meaning yourself.

The above dream is the first in a series of dreams that accompanied therapy related to repressed memories of child abuse. The client achieved a significant level of trust and rapport with the therapist over a period of two or three months, and began to relate incidents of child abuse from the father.

The dream indicates the client's sense of well-being and safety in the present, even though planes are dropping bombs right in front of him. Sulfur signals the beginning of an alchemical process in which both intellect and intuition are available. Therefore, even though the bombs seem like duds, they indicate a shift in consciousness and signal the beginning of the healing process.

In therapeutic situations the initial dream often poses a question critical to the entire process. It is the first direct contact with the unconscious and as such is an auspicious event. It signals the direction in which the unconscious is moving at the time of the dream. Because of this, it offers a complement or contrast to the waking experience and thereby defines the health of the psyche as a whole. A dream that is inconsistent with the waking experience suggests turmoil within the personality. It can reveal the nature of the problem within the unconscious, indicating disagreement between conscious activity and underlying beliefs or feelings. It can foretell psychic impact or affirm your decision or action. It can spotlight some facet of your plan that you may or may not have considered. It can provide a message from your angels, your allies, or from your personal daimon about the decision. (Dreams of the daimon are discussed in chapter 3.)

The way you feel in the initial dream is significant. Sometimes you are excited and filled with pleasant thoughts when you are awake. A dream that has the same feeling tone confirms your waking sentiment. An anxious dream may point to a difficult factor coming up in the future, suggesting the need for attention in your waking life. Only you can examine the feeling and reconcile it to your situation. Any feeling can be a positive indication, depending on how you perceive it.

Generally the unconscious exaggerates to some degree. Often you will chuckle when you identify an extreme emotional reaction in your dream as an exaggerated reflection of a waking life feeling. For example, a little nose drainage from a cold might translate into drowning in a dream, or a pleasant flower arrangement might become a psychedelic experience. The feeling may be tempered as you examine the content of the dream. The dream's tone may also influence your future actions in your waking life.

As you read through this book and begin to record your dreams in the program, you may encounter dream images that are an extension of the initial dream. The program is designed to help you track dream elements easily. Your initial dream may eventually relate to many dreams that you record, as its elements become old friends along the path of your dream life.

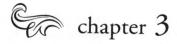 chapter 3

Dreams of the Personal Daimon

The Hair

My hair is much longer. I am amazed at it—it is at least twelve inches longer in the back.

The image is so real that, awake, I check in the mirror to see if it really *is* that long.

From the beginning there is a spark of spirit within you, a daimon, that demands to be heard. This inner voice, sometimes loud, sometimes nearly silent, accompanies you on the path of life and speaks to you when you need a nudge in the right direction. This is the voice that tells you what you want to be when you grow up. It pushes you to achievements you didn't know you were capable of, and steers you away from pursuits that are truly not your cup of tea. It is utterly persistent—relentless even—and will not leave you alone if you are going the wrong way.

The daimon is free to come to you in dreams. It presents maps of the future in which you are fulfilled. It addresses every possible area of concern in order to push you along. Many cultures believe that you choose your path, or lessons, before you are born. It is the daimon that recalls the path and provokes the learning. Life itself provides the lessons. The daimon makes you stick to the lesson until you have learned what you need to know.

In the dream example above, the dreamer's hair is longer. Traditionally longer hair indicates greater strength. Is the daimon saying that the dreamer is stronger? That she needs to become stronger? That she should grow her hair? Only the dreamer can be certain what the message is. It is her dream about her hair. We know the daimon is speaking because the image is of the dreamer herself and her hair. This dream is a message *from* the self *to* the self. In *A Dictionary of Symbols,* Cirlot indicates that "hair on the head, because it grows on the top of the human body, symbolizes spiritual forces . . . In general, hairs represent energy, and are related to the symbolism of levels. That is, a head of hair, being located on the head, stands for higher forces"(1971, 134–35). We may conclude that the daimon is sending a message concerning the dreamer's spiritual development, and is indicating that it has grown. The dream is so powerful that the dreamer checks in the mirror, upon awakening, to see if the growth shows.

The daimon can take on many different forms, and at different stages of life you may have characteristic dream figures who speak to you, cajole you, or literally shove you into the next experience. They may consult with you, or even ask *you* for advice. The daimon will take any form it needs to get your attention.

In *Webster's Ninth New Collegiate Dictionary* the word *daimon* (sometimes spelled *daemon*) is defined under *demon*. Sometimes when your daimon acts you may feel that you are possessed by a demon that forces you in a certain direction regardless of what you think you want. I personally feel that possession by demons is very rare indeed. However, I also believe that if you ignore your inner voice, it will pursue you, ridicule you, and pester you until you listen. It can feel just like a demon.

Webster's also defines *demon* as "a supernatural being of Greek mythology intermediate between gods and men." It is my sense that your daimon is your spirit. As such it may very well be in closer touch with the gods and goddesses than you are in your conscious everyday life. I also believe that the daimon can be carried over from past lives and intermediate lives on other planes, and that it serves as a reservoir of memory of what your soul's true purpose or purposes may be.

When people feel that their soul is lost, it may be that they have lost contact with their daimon—their inner voice. If this happens, it is imperative to re-establish that contact. Sometimes life events cause us to doubt what we have been doing, and we need to listen to the inner voice to find new ground, to show us a new map, to guide us in a new direction. The daimon is always there, no matter how lost you may occasionally feel. It may be silent, but it never dies.

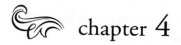 chapter 4

Children's Dreams

The Canal

I am floating in very clear water in a canal like the one a few blocks from my childhood home. It was a ditch lined with concrete, and was actually very clear. Suddenly something—a vine or a piece of wire—wraps around my leg and pulls me under the water. I am unable to escape and believe I will drown.

I did have an incident when I was trapped beneath a very heavy object and thought I might suffocate. I also recall that my best friend's brother wandered up to the ditch, fell in, and drowned. I am sure I heard a very graphic story about the perils of playing around that ditch from my mother.

The Elephant

I am about seven to nine years old in these repetitive dreams. I am at our family's summer cottage. An elephant comes and knocks on the doors and windows, begging to be let in, and my mother keeps saying no. She doesn't see that it is really my father wanting to come in the house, and she thinks it is just an elephant. I am the only one who can tell it is really my dad. I am upset that my mom won't let him in the house.

We stayed at the cottage for the summer and my dad commuted to St. Paul. He would often arrive home very late, after we were in bed, and sometimes he had been drinking, which upset my mother. I remember having this dream several times.

Although not all children's dreams are repetitive, children often tell about a dream that they have over and over. While it is hard to determine whether the dream is exactly the same each time, it is clear that the child believes it is. There are compelling reasons why any person, particularly children, dream repeatedly about the same thing: they are trying to sort out some facet of reality, and the unconscious is assisting in that process. The fact that the dream occurs establishes its relevance. The meaning of the dream is another story. In the case of children, there are at least three obvious reasons for recurrent dreams: (1) to resolve feelings after a traumatic event, (2) to explain environmental conditions during sleep, and (3) to learn and practice developing skills.

Dreams after Trauma

When children experience something painful or frightening, the event is often followed by a series of dreams. The first dream above was a cause of great concern to the child's mother. She knew that something very frightening had happened to cause the nightmare, but she was at a loss as to what it might have been. She even took extra steps to protect the child from drowning. No one remembered anything that could explain the panic the dream evoked. Many years later a conversation with a sibling revealed that their alcoholic father had passed out on top of the dreamer while kissing her goodnight when she was about four years old.

The elephant dream has similar translations of waking world facts into unusual dream elements. The fact that the mother did not want to admit the father into the house translates into nonrecognition. This, combined with the loud footsteps and knocking, produces a clumsy elephant.

Adults have a vast amount of experience to apply to any event that happens in our lives. Usually we are able to draw upon it to resolve fear or other feelings that arise each day. Occasionally something so traumatic happens that we cannot resolve the feelings, and this is when a repetitive dream may occur. We often can see subtle changes happening within the dreams, until finally we dream of a resolution and we don't have the dream again.

Children have relatively little experience upon which to draw. If a trauma occurs, children may replay the event in their minds both during waking hours and during sleep. In itself this replaying does not appear to have value, but it serves the purpose of taking away the shock of the event. Replaying an event in one's mind makes the event more familiar—it ceases to be a one-time occurrence. In the meantime, if a child tells the dream to others, it could draw input that expands the experience base. There may be expressions of caring, scoffing, presentation of additional facts, or other seemingly unrelated events that help the child resolve the problem presented in the recurring dream.

Helen Keller's Dreams

Many of us are familiar with the story of Helen Keller's life. Rendered deaf and blind by an illness at nineteen months, she was an understandably difficult child to raise. Finally her teacher, Anne Sullivan, taught Helen hand signing. Anne tried again and again to create a connection between signing and the meaning of things in Helen's life, but Helen did not make the connection. During the time Anne was Helen's tutor, Helen's mother discovered that Helen signed in her sleep. Finally one day when Helen intentionally spilled a pitcher of water in an angry outburst, Anne dragged her out to the pump to refill the pitcher. She signed water and made Helen pump the water. In that moment Helen connected signing with physical reality, and was able to use the language of signs to make sense of the world.

This is a dramatic story about dreaming because Helen was able to sign in her sleep before she could apply the symbols to her waking life. The dreams in which she signed helped create a world in which language could be used. A similar mental process occurs when children are learning to read. They know the letters before they know how to use them. In general we know and recognize symbols before we consciously understand their archetypal meanings.

We encourage children (and adults) to envision themselves performing an action perfectly. We know that successful athletes run through the coming event in their minds, seeing themselves performing perfectly. We rehearse for speeches and presentations. And no doubt some rehearsal takes place in dreams. Helen Keller provides an example of the depth of such rehearsal. We don't really know what babies dream about, but we know that they dream. Because we understand the essential connection between the outer material world and the inner world of the mind, we can count on the fact that children rehearse meaningful connections between the two worlds in dreams.

Dreams in Which a Skill
Is Being Developed or Mastered

Helen Keller's story is about making the initial conscious connection between meaningful symbols and physical reality. In the case of skill development, children can use dreams in a more direct way. Many times a child will say, "I dreamed that I was a [Fill in the blank with anything: teacher, fireman, basketball star, parent, any role you can imagine.]." The dream is a preview of what it might be like to be an adult. The dreamer is running though the possibilities to find out what feels like a good direction or career. Some children know very early what they want to be when they grow up, and others seem to struggle to find the right path. Dreams provide all the possibilities; a dream's content and the emotion felt in the dream reveal the opinion of the unconscious on the subject.

Do you remember any childhood dreams of what you would be as an adult? If you do, examine them in light of what you are doing now. Do they fit? Do you wish you could have gone down a different path? The dream may have information for you even today.

I suspect that children dream about people talking to them before they learn to speak. Words and phrases are heard during waking and dreaming states thousands of times before a child is able to verbalize recognizable language patterns. Occasionally we hear sleeping babies babbling, and certainly both adults and children sometimes talk in their sleep.

Children's dreams focus on childhood stages of development, just as adults' dreams can indicate adult life changes. We are always growing and changing our understanding of things, and during each stage of development we may have dreams appropriate for that time. It is just as important to consider the dream in the context of the dreamer's age and circumstances as it is to remember that the dream belongs to the dreamer and has personal significance. If a child tells you a dream, remember that the dream is not yours, and cannot be interpreted according to your adult beliefs and feelings. At the same time, remember that you have been entrusted with the knowledge of the dream, and you have the capacity to aid the child's understanding of it. If you teach a child to value and pay attention to dreams, you enrich the child's life.

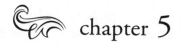 chapter 5

Recurrent Adult Dreams

The Lost Baby

The dream repeats with the details slightly altered. In it I have a baby but I can't find it. Sometimes it is too small to find among the bedclothes. Sometimes I realize that I need to feed it, as I haven't thought of that for several days. Usually the place is familiar. There are baby things around, but no baby in the bed. I am searching a big house with many rooms in some of the dreams.

When I awoke from these dreams I was depressed and sad. In the dream I am anxious and panicky. I feel guilty and I have a sense of profound loss.

Many adults have reported that the same dream comes to them many times, perhaps over a long period of time. The dream may appear identical to the others or it may change slightly. A repeating dream conveys significance—otherwise, why is it repeated? In many cases the dream recurs until its meaning is discovered, and then it changes, fades, or ceases completely.

Carl Jung offered some explanations of recurrent dreams based on the dreams themselves: First, we may be able to infer future events from the dream, provided, of course, that we either recognize a relationship with things likely to occur or have an intuition of presentiment. The second explanation is to look into the past. This only works if the dreamer remembers the past events or is willing to admit to them. Often past events are forgotten or repressed. If there is an association with the past in a dream, it may be time to relieve the repression initially invoked as a protective mechanism. See chapter 4 for more discussion about repetition in children's dreams.

Repetitive dreams present a situation or problem that remains unresolved (in the example above, the dreamer had indeed been separated from her child). The dream reminds you that you are working on this problem in your unconscious as well as waking life. Read about lucid dreaming in chapter 15 to find ways to change your attitude within the dream if it occurs again.

In the example above, the repeating dream was almost exactly the same, time after time. Below is an example of a recurrent dream that has changed over time. The following dream developed as a result of conscious therapy.

More Bombs

I am playing in a sandbox alone, yet I feel very safe. To the west I can see the mountains. They are purple. The sky is clear blue, yet the sunlight is not too intense. The sand is very fine and clean. There are some old-fashioned swings for small children that look sort of like painted crates hanging from two chains. The sides of the sandbox are painted red. There is no sound at all.

I see mushroom clouds sprouting from several locations on or near the mountains. I am curious about this, but not at all afraid. As this happens, the sky seems to darken, but there is no wind or rain.

From an initial dream about planes dropping ineffectual bombs (see chapter 2), the dreamer has progressed to major explosions, representing his anger toward his father. It developed that the bombs were falling on all the places where his father had ever lived. The adult client has been empowered in the dream. He no longer produces dream images of stink bombs, but has graduated to nuclear devices.

There is a distinct element of wish fulfillment in this dream. As a child, the client felt powerless to retaliate against his father. Repression protected him from inexpressible rage. As an adult, he could express his anger in dreams, and then verbalize his feelings. The nuclear weapons speak to the intense force of anger that first emerged only as big fat "stinks."

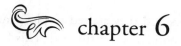 chapter 6

Prophetic Dreams

The Party

I am sitting in a chair in the dining room of my sister's house, looking into the living room. The living room is dark, except for the light coming through the window. I am just looking toward the window when music starts to play. It fills the sky. It is beautiful classical music. Then it stops. A few seconds later it starts again. It plays for five or ten seconds and then stops again. This happens five or six times. After the last time there is another pause and then suddenly thousands of pieces of candy in pretty colored wrappers fall from the sky. Like rain, they land all over the ground. Then all the children of the neighborhood come running outside and run around laughing and screaming and picking up all the pieces of candy.

When I woke up, I had a deep feeling of happiness from this dream. It was so beautiful and colorful. I could not get it out of my mind.

About two weeks after I had the dream, my sister called me and asked if I would come to the birthday party she was having for my nephew, to help with the games and food. I said I would and two weeks after that I went to the party. After the kids played outside for a while, we called them in to play some games. My sister told me to go sit in the dining room, and she would be right in. I sat in a chair against the wall out of the way.

After having sat there for a minute, I realized that this was the chair, in the same place that I was sitting in my dream. I looked into the living room, which was dark, with light coming in the window. At that moment I knew I was "in my dream."

My sister set up some chairs and they started to play "musical chairs." The music came on and filled the room. Then it stopped. This happened five or six times until they had a winner. Then she left the room and came back with a piñata. She hung it up from the ceiling between the dining room and living room, so that I could see it hanging in front of that window. The kids each took a swat at it until someone broke it, and the candy "fell from the sky." The kids all ran around laughing and screaming while they were picking it up.

I had this dream about twelve years ago, and it is still as vivid as ever in my mind.

Wilderness Meeting

I am in the Boundary Waters with my buddy Rocko. Further down the river, I meet up with another friend of mine, Joe, and we manically pursue all kinds of absurd adventures.

When I awoke, I recounted this very vivid dream to Rocko. We had breakfast, broke camp, and headed down the river . . . We noticed canoes coming toward us. It was Joe! This, in a wilderness area of over six million acres, where we may have seen only a dozen other parties in two weeks. Joe and his friends had been canoeing for three weeks.

You may have had dreams that you didn't understand at the time, but later you realized the dream was foretelling something that was about to happen. When you first awoke from the dream, you may have thought it was odd or dismissed it as irrelevant. Later you have to admit that the dream was a picture foretelling something that came to pass.

I feel it is important to remember that not *all* dreams foretell the future. Life would be horrible if you knew that all your dreams would become reality. Dreams sometimes picture how the psyche is wrestling with a problem. They present variations on plots and themes and show us ways to sort and organize the information we have gathered about a problem during the day. Sometimes dreams are silly, improbable ways of sorting, and sometimes they are remarkably accurate assessments. Such dreams do not foretell how things will turn out as much as they just rehash the facts. They do, however, add their own information to the mix, providing the conscious mind with new perspectives and insights.

Prophetic dreams cannot always be identified, but they do have certain characteristics. Traditional psychotherapy would dismiss them as merely anticipatory, while shamans and seers would depend on them for making serious life decisions. You will develop your own style in dealing with them. Some of their characteristics include:

A. Elements seem true

Suddenly thousands of pieces of candy in pretty colored wrappers fall from the sky. Like rain, they land all over the ground. Occasionally dreams seem so real you believe the events have actually occurred. You accept the dream as true even while you perceive that it reflects something that has not happened. While candy does not fall from the sky, it seemed totally believable in the dream. To the dreamer, there is nothing in the dream that seems like a movie or fiction story. Such dreams are said to have an *eidetic* quality—details are remembered in extremely accurate detail. This quality is also shared with epic and psychic dreams, but it does not occur in all cases. It is possible that some déjà vu experiences are the result of very detailed dreams that come true.

B. Elements have their own internal logic

We manically pursue all kinds of absurd adventures. You might see how the events of a prophetic dream are reasonable, logical outcomes of current circumstances known to you. Or, although the dream may seem improbable to you upon awaking, no part of it violates its internal consistency. In the above case, meeting the second friend was highly unlikely and the following adventures were no more so in the context of the dream.

C. Events have meaning for you

I am sitting on a chair in the dining room of my sister's house, looking into the living room. Prophetic dreams have meaning for you personally. They may not be about you, but they will involve people or places you know. When you have the dream you may not understand the association, but it is there nonetheless. Thus a dream of events on the other side of the world is an outgrowth of your interest in international politics, or the pattern of news reports you have heard, or some other part of your present reality. Most prophetic dreams have to do with close family or associates, or the region of the world you live in, and are therefore associated with your normal sphere of experience.

D. Numinosity

Music starts to play. It fills the sky. It is beautiful classical music. Then it stops. A few seconds later it starts again. Certain dreams have a compelling quality that causes you to remember them in great detail. They seem to vibrate with a life of their own. Prophetic dreams often have this quality. The word *numinous* means supernatural or mysterious, filled with a sense of the divine or spiritual. Such a dream is more than the ordinary nightly dream—it takes on a larger significance.

Waking Visions Concerning the Future

Premonitions can take the form of waking visions. Historically it was believed that visions were not bidden, but came to individuals either directly from the Deity or from some evil source. Saints who had visions were often tested and often thought to be possessed by some "devil." The vision quest of the American Indians is one example of the significance of seeking help in the form of a personal vision, and was a fairly common practice. Most dreams come of their own accord and not as a result of a conscious desire to have them.

Modern shamanic and psychological theories suggests we can ask for dreams or visions. Vision quests are perhaps physically less rigorous than they once were, but the value of exploring the world through a vision remains part of the ritual. Many people today successfully call upon dreams. They develop a ritual in which they specify the question they are seeking to answer and then await a dream response. This creates a climate of acceptance by dampening the fearful resistance of what might be seen and grounding the wild desires to see something specific. Thus, through the ritual of appeal, the transmission of a dream is purified to the quality of a vision direct from the source.

A Monk's Dream

It is said that in the fourteenth century a Chinese monk had a dream in which he saw the Forbidden City completed. He felt deeply moved by it, and near the year A.D. 1400 he told Yung Lo, a prince.

Yung Lo later took the name Black Dragon, declared himself emperor, and was determined to build the city according to the monk's detailed dream. He gathered people and resources and spent years on the project. It is said that the people even erected a mountain to provide the proper *feng shui* for the site. Yung Lo died before the city was completed.

Joan of Arc's Vision

The monk lived at about the same time as Joan of Arc. Joan was a simple peasant girl who had visions of how to defeat the British enemies of the realm, and she was so certain of her vision that she was able to convince Charles VII, the king, to let her lead the French army into battle. Her vision included enough information to help her develop a complex strategic plan that led to victory.

Both the Chinese monk and Joan of Arc had extraordinary dream and visionary experiences. The nature of the two experiences fits the format of a prophetic dream precisely:

1. In both cases the experience seemed true. Neither person doubted that the experience was momentous, and both acted on the dream or vision. Both had good reason to think that the experiences were highly unlikely, but both acted in spite of that.

2. Both experiences had their own internal logic. For the monk, the logic included a nearly celestial city so perfectly designed that the *chi* (physical and spiritual energy of space) flowed properly in every respect. It was gloriously large and beautifully appointed—a true seat for the emperor. Joan saw herself at the head of an army, but she also saw every detail of a battle plan that she was certain would work.

3. Both experiences had intense meaning. The monk knew he had dreamed of a perfect palace for the divine emperor, and Joan knew she had seen the perfect way to defeat an enemy. Both went out of their ordinary life path to communicate their experience to a higher authority.

4. Both experiences had the requisite numinous quality. Neither the monk nor Joan could forget their experience, and neither could avoid following through with it.

I should note at this point that not all prophetic dreams require or even allow the dreamer to take appropriate action. Where the monk and Joan had experiences that were eventually manifested in physical reality, many prophetic dreams seem to give us advance warning without suggesting action of any kind on our part. Many people dream of the injury or death of loved ones and are unable to do anything to prevent the accident or illness. This can be the source of great sorrow and guilty feelings. We wish we could do something to prevent or change the outcome.

When you feel you have had a prophetic dream or vision in your waking life, it can be very useful to tell someone else about it. The act of telling someone provides the opportunity to review the dream out loud. By telling someone about the dream you can also evaluate its power. If the other person remains unmoved or provides a rational explanation for the dream that you have overlooked, your feelings may be put to rest. On the other hand, if the person takes the dream very seriously and finds a way to apply it to the future or suggests appropriate action, you have found confirmation in the waking world. Keep in mind that the reaction of another person can be erroneous or disingenuous. A reaction also depends on who you ask—a rationalist versus an alarmist, for example—and which interpretation you want to hear.

Telling someone about an event that may happen in the future can take the place of direct intervention on your part. The telling itself may be a form of duty fulfillment. By telling the dream to someone you may have an indirect effect on events, in harmony with right action, and without the ego's intention to prevent something.

The more subtle benefit of telling someone about a prophetic dream is that you acknowledge your unconscious mind and its capacity to provide meaningful information. Each time you do this, you make friends with your deep inner source. As with any talent, the more you acknowledge and work with your capacity for meaningful dreams, the more they will flow.

You may simply record the dream and analyze it carefully. As you gain experience using the dream journal program, you will find that your dreams become rich and alive with meaning, and that the meaning carries over into your daily life. You can also record any visions or important episodes, as you would in a diary, and use the program to examine them. Over a period of time you will find that to some extent the waking images parallel your dreams. By tracking both you will gain a richer insight into your self and your spiritual path and you will gain confidence to use your intuitive abilities more fully.

How Dreams Affect the Future (and Vice Versa)

Because the prophetic dream occurs before an event, we can sometimes change the future. When we dream of someone having an accident, we may be able to prevent an injury because we "know" what is about to happen. However, knowing what will happen is sometimes part of causing it to happen.

Banana Sandwiches

I am making my tea, which is mostly comprised of banana sandwiches. Then the phone rings and it is my boyfriend's best friend who explains that my boyfriend has just had an accident. [He] has fallen off his motorcycle and is now in the hospital. My response is not, as might be expected, concern, depression, or to ask many questions as to how he is. It is the wholly inappropriate remark, "Oh yes!" and to burst into laughter.

I told my boyfriend and his friend and they smiled. However, a few hours later, after I returned home, I was indeed making banana sandwiches when the phone rang and—sure enough—it is my boyfriend's best friend speaking the exact words from my dream. Without thinking, I said, "Oh yes!" and began to laugh, convinced that they were playing a practical joke on me. But they were not. What he was telling me was the truth. (Randles 1994, 93)

This dream shows how we can play with the reality of time. The dreamer first had the dream, in which she laughed inappropriately. Then the incident occurred, in which she thought her boyfriend was playing a joke on her. Although the friend had forgotten the dream he had been told, she remembered, and that is why she laughed about it. However, she had laughed about it before the event in her dream, and that was, in fact, what caused her to laugh in waking life!

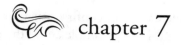

chapter 7

Balance and Confirmation in Dreams

The House

I am in my house cleaning, and my counselor is helping by cleaning the cupboards. I go to get a broom or mop, and I find two new rooms I didn't know I had. They are bright and sunny and large. I am dragging the wet mop, leaving a trail. I call the two boys to come look. I feel great joy.

Upon awakening, I felt great joy. I realized I could handle the life situation I was facing—the two rooms were for the boys, and I knew I could take care of both of them.

There were other dreams where the rooms were too crowded. They showed ways to rearrange things.

The balancing dream represents the psyche's attempt to bring the mental state back into harmony. Such a dream acts as a counterbalance to waking activities that have taken you away from your normal path. When analyzing balancing dreams, it is important to recognize early on that the dream is not predicting likely actions in the waking world. Rather it is providing a contrasting set of circumstances and feelings. The unconscious mind, not having the capacity for logical deductive reasoning, provides what it *is* capable of—inductive logic. In the above case it provides its version of the alternative course of action.

Confirmation in dreams shows a very different purpose. Some dreams appear to be balancing dreams but are actually confirming what you have concluded in waking consciousness. In the balancing dream the content is opposite to your waking life. In the dream of confirmation the content is very similar to waking life, and confirms that you are going in the right direction. Such a dream confirms that your conscious analysis of the situation is accurate and balanced. In the example above the dreamer finds rooms in a house for her children and room in her psyche to manage the challenge of raising them.

The more extreme the waking circumstances, the more extreme the balancing or compensating quality of the dream. If balancing dreams are ignored then the unconscious may add power to the dream content to get our attention. This process, called *enantiodromia,* involves a dream's escalation of images and emotions with the purpose of getting our attention. If you have a series of escalating dream emotions, it is important to take stock of your waking life and discover your true feelings—feelings that may not align with your moral value system.

Balancing dreams provide a golden opportunity to make friends with your unconscious. By acknowledging the embarrassment provoked by such a dream, you take a step toward understanding your deepest motivations more clearly. When your waking actions are closely aligned with your unconscious values, you awake with the feeling of satisfaction. The dream confirms that you are on the right path—that an uncharacteristic handling of a situation fulfilled your purpose on both the conscious and unconscious levels.

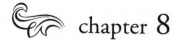

chapter 8

Epic Dreams

Nebuchadnezzar's Dreams

Nebuchadnezzar had dreams that upset him very much and he called upon his magicians and soothsayers to interpret the dreams for him. When they were unable to interpret them satisfactorily, the king called upon Daniel because he was thought to be possessed by the spirit of the holy gods.

> "*Here is the vision which came into my head as I was lying upon my bed:*
>   *As I was looking,*
> *I saw a tree of great height at the centre of the earth;*
>   *the tree grew and became strong,*
>   *reaching with its top to the sky*
>   *and visible to earth's farthest bounds.*
>   *Its foliage was lovely,*
>   *And its fruit abundant;*
>   *and it yielded food for all.*
>   *Beneath it the wild beasts found shelter,*
>   *the birds lodged in its branches,*
>   *and from it all living creatures fed.*
>
> "*Here is another vision which came into me head as I was lying upon my bed:*
>   *As I was watching, there was a Watcher [an angel],*
>   *a Holy One coming down from heaven.*
>   *He cried aloud and said,*

'Hew down the tree, lop off the branches,
strip away the foliage, scatter the fruit.
   Let the wild beasts flee from its shelter
     and the birds from its branches,
but leave the stump with its roots in the ground.
   So, tethered with an iron ring,
   let him eat his fill of the lush grass;
   let him be drenched with the dew of heaven
   and share the lot of the beasts in their pasture;
   let his mind cease to be a man's mind,
   and let him be given the mind of a beast.
   Let seven times pass over him.
   The issue has been determined by the Watchers
   and the sentence pronounced by the Holy Ones.
   Thereby the living will know that the Most High is sovereign in the kingdom of
men: he gives the kingdom to whom he will and he may set over it the humblest of
mankind.'"

(Daniel 4:10–17 New English Bible)

Some dreams are so huge, so compelling, and so vivid that you cannot ignore them. They latch onto you and you remember details that ordinarily would slip back into the unconscious as the day progresses. These epic dreams remain with you for years, as vivid as though they occurred just last night. Such dreams have the following characteristics:

A. Epic dreams have an organization or plot that flows like all epic stories. When you talk about them you are telling a story. The dreams have symmetry or beauty that colors your description. Even grim content fascinates you, like a Cecil B. De Mille spectacular.

B. Epic dreams may contain archetypal material—symbols, characters, or events that extend beyond your personal, ordinary life and connect you to the larger human experience in a profound way. Within the legendary or historical scope of the dream you may feel a sense of awe and forget yourself, momentarily made small by proportion. Conversely, like Nebuchadnezzar, the dream may be your life and its relationship to the whole writ large, and you may behold the thunder of destiny.

Interpreting Nebuchadnezzar's Dreams

Daniel interpreted the dreams to mean that Nebuchadnezzar needed to acknowledge the Most High God. Until that was done, the king would lose his mind and be as an animal. Once he finally recognized God, the king would be restored to his full mental capacity and to his throne as well. Daniel's interpretation did indeed come to pass. But while it is sometimes possible for a psychic or therapist to interpret a dream correctly, the dreamer is generally the best possible interpreter of its meaning.

Let us examine Nebuchadnezzar's dreams and see what we can find out from them. The most prominent elements of his two dreams include:

1. The tree, at first strong enough to support all living creatures easily.
2. The Watcher, or Holy One, sent from heaven to decree.
3. The decree itself.
4. The seven years to follow.
5. The stump and the tether.

Daniel interpreted the tree as symbolic of the king. The upper part of the tree reflects the physical manifestation of a being in the world. The roots, extending into the earth, reflect the unconscious mind of the individual. In the dream the tree is at first supremely powerful, suggesting the king has an overblown opinion of himself.

The Watcher delivers a spiritual message and could be a spirit guide, goddess, or angel. The decree explicitly explains what will happen. The dreamer and the broken remains of his former self will be tethered to the stump of the tree. The tether links him to his "roots." Even though he lost sight of his path, the dreamer remains connected to his human roots.

As an astrologer I find the seven years prediction interesting as this is one-quarter of the period of the planet Saturn. When Saturn moves one-fourth of the way around the zodiac, individuals are offered the chance to evaluate their actions and make changes in their behavior. In this case the decree is for seven years of hard lessons concerning the true nature of the spiritual realm.

Where instincts are represented as inferior in Nebuchadnezzar's dreams, I believe we should not overlook our instincts and stick exclusively to reason. The message of the dreams is that reason cannot be everything and arrogance can cause one's downfall. Only by experiencing the instinctual realm could the king come to understand his true place in the universe. Whether we accept Daniel's interpretation or not, we can certainly relate to the importance of a balanced psyche.

As you begin working with the program, you may recall epic dreams from the past and record them. In so doing, consider whether they had an influence on your life. You may want to record associations to the dream that developed later. Relevant events close to the time of the dream are key confirmations. Events or people who remind you of the dream are also important; you can consider what about them connects to the dream.

The epic dream can be the voice of the daimon setting you on your course in life. Pay attention to each detail of this map of your future. There is often a cyclical quality to epic dreams. Milestones will develop over time to show you where you are in achieving your physical, mental, emotional, and spiritual goals. In such dreams a number of conscious decisions are challenged by plausible, inevitable, prophetic, or "worst case" scenarios. A kind of siege is enacted to test the castle walls and review your progress. In this sense epic dreams seem preparatory, warning, and confirmational.

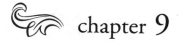 chapter 9

Spotlight Dreams

The Spider

I am in bed. I see a large spider-like creature moving rapidly across the ceiling above me.

When I woke, I could still see it moving, and I woke my wife and said, "You've got to see this." I pointed to the creature on the ceiling, which then started to lose substance, going from three-dimensional to flat, and finally fading away. Of course my wife saw nothing unusual.

Sometimes you have a dream that focuses on one aspect of your life, or one person, or one event. As far as the dream is concerned, this is the only significant thing in your life. The dream provides a glorious moment in which you have only to consider one thing. Like a spotlight on a stage performance, the dream provides the opportunity to focus on one aspect of your life so that you can consider it in isolation from other concerns.

Such a focus can aid in the resolution of problems. Life is so full of desires, needs, and concerns that you can't always focus on one thing. The spotlight dream allows you to concentrate as children do—examine that dandelion of a problem in all its colorful details, inhale its scent, and listen to its message.

The spotlight dream can arrive within the context of other dreams, like a cameo performance in the middle of a drama. There may be a scene within a dream, for example, amid a tangled progression of dreams concerning childhood experiences that reveals the solution to a problem in your waking life.

I once dreamed that my younger brother's hand was found beneath my pillow, severed from his body. This is a grim dream image and I was very anxious in the dream and when I awoke. In reality my brother suffered a terrible accident when he was about eleven years old and his hand was badly damaged. I was told that the surgeon considered amputation during the reconstructive surgery. While I remember this spotlight dream very clearly, I have now forgotten its original context. For me today, the dream points to one kind of choice—to remove something from one's life or to remove one's self from a situation—a decision I often postpone making for as long as possible. The dream reminds me of the possibility of amputating something from my life and my waking memory reminds me that such a choice, while not the only one, or even the best one, is certainly valid.

A spotlight dream may be gloriously satisfying. Many people report a dream in which they are receiving the highest honor their profession has to offer. Such a dream suggests that success is possible. It also informs us that the dream ego sees us as already successful. A person deeply engaged in a life-changing process dreams of the metamorphosis of a butterfly. The dream is unusually vivid, with every detail visible as it would be in bright light under a magnifying glass. The beautiful reality of changing from a fuzzy caterpillar into a monarch butterfly assures one of his or her capacity to get through a difficult time.

Occasionally a parent will have a dream in which an unborn child comes to tell the parent his or her name. The spotlight is focused so poignantly on this new family member that the name is adopted without question.

In the example above, the spider is the only image of any significance and it is compelling enough to remain visible upon awakening. Here is the entry from the dictionary in Part II concerning the spider:

> Spiders have played a role in mythology around the world. The Spider Woman provides the creative impulse to weave for American Indians, and was associated with weaving for the ancient Greeks as well. The spider has several symbolic meanings: First, it has the power to create, indicated by its web. Second, it is aggressive in the treatment of its prey. Third, the pattern of the web is reminiscent of the spiral of life, a profound symbol of progressive development. Hindus thought the spider wove the web of *maya,* or illusion. The thread of life and death symbolizes the pattern of rebirth.

Spotlight dreams are all about your personal spotlight, and as such have intensely personal meaning. The above dictionary extract serves to illuminate the spider image and may provide insight into its significance for the dreamer. Whatever is in the spotlight, it has very high value to the dreamer even if it may seem relatively tame to other people.

chapter 10

Animal Dreams

The Panther

There is a black panther pacing through my house. I am afraid, yet fascinated.

This was one in a series of dreams.

I find that I have given birth to four tiny kittens of different colors. They are so helpless and I don't know how to take care of them. I put them in a white enamel dish and warm them with a lamp. I wonder how I will feed them, and I call loudly for help.

Some years after the dream, I have a mother cat who dies and leaves two kittens. I go to the veterinarian to get kitten food and a tiny bottle, with which I feed the kittens.

Animal helpers come to us in dreams and visions as well as in our daily lives. They provide a profound connection to the spirit world and show us, by their traits, how we can manifest creative energy in our lives. While certain animals are associated with specific signs of the zodiac and are therefore personally powerful, any animal can appear to you.

Awake, you can call upon a specific animal to provide its special guidance. In dreams, however, the animal chooses to come to you. Thus a dream animal is a powerful symbol of your instinctual nature, as well as the animal's own intelligence. The example dreams above were my own and they provoked me to study the nature of the panther. The dreams also caused me to realize the helplessness of my own spirit to thrive without my conscious help, and to consider the ways I can interact with the world around me when I am afraid.

I was not feeling especially strong when I had the panther dreams, in fact I was feeling quite the opposite. The dreams provided a focus for my thoughts and showed me I had the inner strength I sought. In *Animal-Speak,* Ted Andrews states, "Individuals with panthers as totems are usually individuals who came into the world with the [inner] lights already on. Thus they should not be discouraged when they do not experience what others describe . . . They should trust their thoughts and their inner visions (imaginings) because there is probably a strong foundation in reality" (1993, 295). He goes on to say that such individuals may develop *clairaudience*—they hear communications of other dimensions and other life forms.

The black panther's strength is greatest in water, winter, and in the cycle of the new moon. I was born in winter, within two days of the new moon, and water signs figure strongly in my astrological chart. "The black panther is the symbol of the feminine, the dark mother, the dark of the moon. It is often a symbol of darkness, death and rebirth out of it" (Andrews 1993, 297).

Much more could be said about the panther. A detailed study of any animals that appear in your dreams can be a valuable source of information about yourself and your inner strengths. One of the most interesting things I have found is that even seemingly timid, powerless animals have strong wisdom. You may dream about a rabbit and identify with its fear, but you should also consider its other attributes. You can identify with the rabbit's capacity to create a secure, safe home environment in which you can feel protected. The rabbit also has the intelligence to evade an attacker by doubling back on its own trail, by becoming nearly invisible when it is still, and by reading surrounding signs. Finally, the rabbit is fertile, and shows that you are filled with ideas that may be birthed into material reality.

While the rabbit may not take a leadership role, he or she may serve as an active helper, pointing out the signs along the path. The panther may be a loner by choice, but can also provide the strong leadership of the cat family. Whatever your dream animal is, it comes to tell you about your own inner strength and purpose.

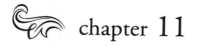 chapter 11

Physical Dreams

Physical Dream

I am with my lover and I am very aware of him as a sexual being. Then I become aware of a third presence in the room, who I think is my child.

I awake and observe that the sound in the dream is actually the breeze blowing the streamers on a kite hanging on the wall, and not my child.

Some dreams are reflections of physical conditions around you. If you are hungry during sleep, the dream may indicate that. If there is a thunderstorm, some of its lights and sounds may be incorporated into your dreams. If your foot falls asleep, it may be "asleep" in your dream. Because of physical body cycles, certain hours of the night might be favorable for certain dreams to appear related to that type of energy. For example, the body typically slows between 3:00 and 5:00 A.M., awake or asleep, and you may feel chilled, with that feeling reflected in your dream as a result.

Other dreams indicate a physical problem that needs attention. After my jaw was broken in a car accident, I dreamed of my teeth becoming loose and falling out. This dream varied in intensity for a period of time, but always with the same result. I was worried because the dream had the qualities of a prophetic dream. Later I had some dental surgery and one tooth had to be removed. After that the dream ceased.

Naturally, not all dreams of loose, breaking, or rotting teeth foretell dental problems. Teeth can be a symbol of aggression and if yours are loose in a dream, it may mean you are feeling a loss of power and could benefit from taking on a more assertive role in your daily life. You may even find that you associate one particular tooth with some facet of your life and that this association bears no resemblance to other people's experience. Teeth, as with all dream symbols, are for you to interpret for yourself.

The Green Room

I dream that I am discussing with a woman about how in my dreams I have a color bias, that I only see blue. She says she can do this thing where I can see all the colors, more vividly than I do when I am awake.

Then I am at a gazebo made of stuff like the treehouse in The Swiss Family Robinson. *On a table there is a wooden carving of Lono or a similar Hawaiian god. I walk across the room. There is a ledge where you can look down on a green pool with things growing in it. The light is green. The pool looks abandoned. The whole space is covered with green plants and mold and weird things.*

A woman speaks to me. I ask why the color I am seeing is green and she says, "Those are the rules of the game." I say, "I can't believe how green everything is. It's great—it's really really green. But it is also the only color I can see. Why is that?"

This scene from a longer dream is focused entirely on the color green and the dreamer's amazement at its depth and richness. Green is associated with the heart chakra, so we can conclude that the dreamer is focusing in some new way on heart energy, since usually she is more focused on blue (throat chakra). Green is also associated with effective action in Buddhist psychology, so we can further conclude that the dreamer's actions are being confirmed for her through the dream. But the fun of this dream is in the color's power to completely flood perception.

chapter 12

Spirit or Message Dreams

My Aunt

My aunt, who had Down's syndrome, would rock and sing to my older sister all day long. My aunt had tremendous patience, and nothing my sister did ever upset or tired her. My mother always said it was as if my aunt had found someone who needed her, that she could take care of. My aunt died while my sister was still a baby. One night my mother had the following dream:

My dead sister is leaning over my bed, shaking me and telling me to wake up. "The baby, the baby," she keeps crying.

The dream finally woke my mother up, and she decided that since she was awake, she would check on the baby. She went into the nursery, where she found my sister struggling with the baby blanket wrapped around her neck.

Just a Message

A voice says, "You are in danger."

This is the entire dream.

I will examine the second dream first. The message itself is quite clear. The dreamer had had message dreams before in which there was only a voice, so she knows that such dreams are important. At the time of this dream there did not appear to be any immediate danger, but nevertheless she felt the dream was significant. How can you work with a dream like this one?

First, I suggest you take such a dream seriously. Your inner voice, angel, or guide is speaking to you. After having such a dream I would recommend a bit of extra caution in your daily activities. Naturally, if you are a counterspy on a deadly mission you already know you are in a dangerous situation. If you are living a more mundane existence, on the other hand, you will want to be careful when you are going to your car in a dark, downtown parking lot, and you will want to pay attention to what you are doing when you work with sharp knives. You will also want to watch your step when you go up and down steep stairs.

Second, remember that the unconscious does not have a moderation dial. When the unconscious identifies a bit of anger, it can magnify the anger into a gun battle or even a nuclear explosion. A little icy patch by the front door can be expressed in a dream as a much larger problem. Thus the dream message "You are in danger," can be an exaggerated message concerning something less dramatic.

Third, if you have a health condition that you monitor regularly, you may want to get a checkup. If you have been eating foods not on your diet, you may want to cut back. Maybe you just need to clean your refrigerator and get rid of something too old, or have your well water tested. The dream can be telling you to bring some area of your life back into balance.

Fourth, you might as well continue living your life on a normal basis, but incorporate some degree of caution. After all, the dream could mean a tree branch will fall in your yard in a high wind. You may not even be at home when it happens.

The first dream needs little explanation. The fact that this dream was remembered years later reflects the power of the message. The dreamer had no doubt the message was real. Skeptics might say the mother heard the baby struggling and created the dream in order to arouse herself. I prefer to believe that the baby's aunt was watching over her and sought help when it was needed.

Dreams about spirit guides are generally rather rare. Most people are not so in touch with their spirit guides and angels that they receive messages very often, although a few people are closely in tune on this level. As you work with your dreams you may find yourself beginning to discover meaningful messages that seem to come from outside yourself. I believe our guides and angels can speak to us while we are awake, and certainly while we are asleep.

How can you identify such a message? If you know you have personal angels or guides, then you will know when they appear in a dream because they will look and sound familiar to you. The messenger may even speak about his or her role directly.

If you believe you have had a message dream but you can't identify the source or the meaning, you can ask for clarification the next night. Focus your mind on your angel or guide and ask for what you need. Say something like, "I had a very curious dream last night in which 'x' occurred. I desire to understand 'x' more fully. Please come to me again tonight in a dream and help me understand 'y' [perhaps a particular person or symbol in the dream]." Then search whatever dreams you have for clarification. Even if the dreams seem unrelated to each other, something in them may provide your answer.

One thing is certain about dreams: they can be trusted as messages from your own unconscious mind. You may not always understand them, but they are yours. Some dreams are harder to accept than others. Still, as you work with them, dreams can become an accepted, friendly part of your life. It may be weeks, months, or even years before you fully understand dream elements.

The Spirit Guide

When I was in art school, I had a series of dreams that came on four consecutive nights at the end of a quarter of study. The dreams themselves were not related, except that at the end of each one an American Indian approached me and shook my hand, and then walked away. The handshake seemed to put more meaning into the rest of the dream and helped me notice things about the dream that I might otherwise have missed. The gesture made me feel better about what happened in each dream.

Dream 1
I am outside on a calm, green and blue summer day. But a young boy near a fence injured his hand (palm) badly. I tried to help him as much as I could, but I felt that I didn't know how I could. It bothered me. Then the Indian came, shook my hand, and I felt better.

Dream 2
I am in an art museum, seriously examining art, and feeling a bit critical. The Indian showed up, shook my hand, and suddenly everything about the art made sense.

Dream 3
I am witnessing a rape. Then I am pursued by the rapist, feeling extremely threatened. The Indian appears, shakes my hand, and I am filled with peace and understanding of the troubles of the rapist.

Dream 4

The only thing I remember about the dream is the Indian shaking my hand. This dream occurred after I had spent an entire day blindfolded, in order to understand blindness better. I went to an art museum with a friend during the day and to a psychic circle that evening where they prayed that I would regain my eyesight. I thought it odd that they believed I was really blind. The next morning I got a phone call from the American Society for the Blind, asking if I wanted to give money for the cause! Of course I did.

The following day was the last day of the quarter. As I was leaving one of my classes, an American Indian approached me. He was in the class, but I didn't know anything about him. He was quiet and never associated with anyone. He put out his hand to shake mine. I shook his hand and he said, "I'm glad I got to know you," and then walked away—exactly as it was done in my dreams. I stood there with my mouth wide open, watching him walk down the hallway. I always felt inadequate as an artist up to that moment, but then all of a sudden I was filled with peace and understanding.

Later that night at a party, I made a thin braid of my hair and cut it off—I felt compelled to do this. I was holding it in my hand and another American Indian approached me and told me he had noticed my art and felt bad that he never got to know me. I handed him the braid. He more or less knelt before me and said he was honored to have been given such a gift.

It turned out that the two Indians were brothers and didn't know that the other had spoken to me. Still later I went to a psychic. After the reading I told her about the Indian in my dreams and she said, "He is one of your spirit guides."

This series of dreams and waking activities reveals how elements of day and night activities combine together to tell an important story for the dreamer. Because of this story, which occurred at the completion of a quarter of study, the dreamer gained personal confidence, experienced a bit of the unknown, received and gave powerful compliments, and confirmed that she had met one of her spirit guides. Before our guides can come to us, we need an open heart and mind.

The next chapter is about psychic dreams. Psychic dreams are similar to spirit dreams, but with one striking difference: in spirit dreams someone comes to you, while in psychic or astral dreams you go to the scene of the dream yourself.

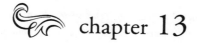 chapter 13

Psychic and Astral Dreams

John F. Kennedy Jr.

I need to find JFK Jr. and my guides light a way for me to get to him. It is very bright and I can see my way to him. He is still in the cockpit of the plane.

I introduce myself to him and tell him that I am there to get him and bring him to the light. I communicate this telepathically. He knows he is dead, but says that he isn't ready to go. He says that he feels guilty and responsible and feels that he has killed the others. I reassure him that accidents happen, that they are already there [in the light] and waiting for him.

After a period of time he goes with me and we follow the light. When we reach the surface of the water, I stay at the surface and he continues up his path.

Then I woke up. The clock said 3:07 A.M. CDT, July 21, 1999. CNN reported that morning that JFK Jr.'s body was found between 2:00 and 2:30 A.M. EST.

I was very moved by this dream and didn't go back to sleep for a couple of hours afterwards. I was very at peace. When I woke up [the next] morning, I knew that he had been found and was OK.

Shelley's Dream Recollection

I was walking with a friend, in the neighborhood of that city, engaged in earnest and interesting conversation. We suddenly turned the corner of a lane, and the view, which its high banks and hedges had concealed, presented itself. The view consisted of a wind-mill, standing in one among many plashy meadows, inclosed with stone walls; the irregular and broken ground, between the wall and the road on which we stood; a long

49

low hill behind the windmill, and a grey covering of uniform cloud spread over the evening sky. It was that season when the last leaf had just fallen from the scant and stunted ash. The scene surely was a common scene; the season and the hour little calcu-lated to kindle lawless thought; it was a tame uninteresting assemblage of objects, such as would drive the imagination for refuge in serious and sober talk, to the evening fire-side, and the dessert of winter fruits and wine. The effect which it produced on me was not such as could have been expected. I suddenly remembered to have seen that exact scene in some dream of long [ago] . . . Here I was obliged to leave off, overcome by thrilling horror. (Shelley 1951, 476)

I have chosen to discuss psychic and astral dreams together because it is often difficult to determine which is which. The psychic dream makes you aware of events that are occur-ring outside the range of your ordinary senses. An example would be a dream in which you see or hear something that is happening thousands of miles away as if you are listen-ing to the radio or watching a movie. An astral dream is one in which you leave your body and travel to a distant location. In an astral dream you sense you are somewhere else, even though your body remains asleep. It may be difficult to distinguish between these two types of dreams. One way is to determine where you are in the dream. Are you in your bed, or in your own house, but aware of events occurring outside your range of senses? If so, you are having a psychic dream. Are you in some distant location—perhaps a place you have never actually seen? Are you in a place that violates the laws of science and physics? Are you in the past or future? If so, you are having an astral dream.

It is sometimes possible to confirm details of a dream. If you see a certain person in a dream, you can contact him or her in waking life and relate the dream. If the dream includes a specific event, you may hear later that the event occurred the way you dreamed it. In the first example above, confirmation occurred within a very short period of time. Sometimes you have to wait longer for confirmation, or you may never receive it at all. If you dream about a place you have never visited and then visit it at a later date, you may recall the dream or you may simply feel a sense of déjà vu. Shelley's example demonstrates this. I have found that acknowledging déjà vu feelings helps promote their recurrence, as it demonstrates respect for the work of the unconscious.

Psychic events generally occur at or near the time you have the dream. For example, the Dalai Lama recalled a dream in which he experienced the destruction of a distant Tibetan village by the Chinese during an invasion of his country. As he dreamt of it, the event was actually happening. Psychic dreams may occur because of a close emotional link between you and the dream characters or places. There is often a discernable reason for the dream. Swedenborg's vision, described in the next chapter, also had personal relevance, but he was awake at the time the vision occurred.

By contrast, the astral dream may occur in a very different reality. The astral realm affects senses other than your usual ones—colors, the flow of time, the shape of objects, and the nature of other entities may all be very different from ordinary experience. This realm may contain entities that are projections of your own beliefs. If you expect to see scary beings, you will see them. Emotions also have a large effect on the appearance of this realm. Because of this, astral dreams can be directed using the lucid dreaming process (see chapter 15). You can decide where you are going and with whom, and the astral realm accommodates.

Recognizing the differences between psychic dreams and astral dreams may be important. If you are aware you are dreaming, remain unable to affect the dream, and all the dream elements appear to be normal in a mundane sense, then the dream is more likely psychic. If the dream elements are subject to skewed rules of logic, if you are aware you are dreaming, and you are able to change the appearance of things, then you may be having an astral dream, or at least a lucid one. A psychic dream reveals information about the physical plane that you could not normally know. An astral dream is an experience that involves movement in or through the astral plane. The difference between the two is important because one dream—the psychic—provides information, while the other—the astral—provides personal experience. In either case, analyzing the dream experience tells you about yourself in relation to the dream content.

chapter 14

Waking Dreams and Visions

Swedenborg's Remote Viewing

On the Saturday evening of July 19th, 1759, [Emanuel] Swedenborg was one of sixteen guests invited to the home of his friend William Castell in Gothenburg, which is 240 miles from Stockholm. Swedenborg was enjoying dinner with the other guests when he suddenly beheld a stark vision of a massive blaze raging in Stockholm. He told the bemused guests around the table about the fiery vision and became pallid and greatly agitated. He left the house for a breath of fresh air and returned with more details which disturbed a number of the guests. He told one person present that his house had been totally destroyed by the fire and that his own house was now threatened by the hungry flames. He described vividly the course and extent of the raging fire, then suddenly at 8 P.M. he slumped in a chair out of breath and sighed, "Thank God. The fire is extinguished, the third door from my house."

Many of the guests were still skeptical, but on Monday evening, a messenger arrived from Stockholm and confirmed every detail of Swedenborg's account of the blaze. (Slemen 1998, 290)

Swedenborg was able to tell the authorities exactly how the fire began.

Perhaps no single personal event is as compelling as a waking dream or vision. Throughout recorded history we find examples that hold our attention. The oracle at Delphi, seemingly through the agency of mind-altering gases venting from the depths of the earth, was able to foretell the future. LSD and other psychotropic drugs reveal layers of reality that our ordinary senses cannot perceive. Moses and the prophets saw and heard the Lord and carried his message to their followers. Ancient Greek and European stories record encounters with gods or goddesses in great detail. Saints around the world have had visions of the Virgin or other visitations. All of these occur while the individuals are fully awake.

Some visions are dismissed as psychotic episodes. Schizophrenia is defined in part by the voices one hears when other people hear nothing. Many of us have been taught to ignore any sensory input that deviates from what other people perceive. And how would we determine if a vision is real or simply a delusion? One way to gauge this is to ask whether the vision is inconsistent with other known facts. Generally the only inconsistency is that other people cannot see it. The rest of the details are consistent with ordinary experience, the laws of physics, and so on. Delusions are marked by fantastic qualities or highly improbable outcomes. They can fluctuate from one wild idea to another, pictorially reflecting the whims of strong but unfocused emotions. Or delusions can also fixate on one thing. Swedenborg's vision would have been a delusion, except that the events happened precisely when and as he described them. Visions are more likely to break a dam and cause a flood of emotion; they are illuminating and startling, but incisive.

I recall having a waking vision. I was sitting at my desk working when it began, and I am certain I didn't move or speak for a number of minutes, perhaps fifteen. The sum total of the vision's content was a door.

The door was locked with a huge, brightly polished lock that had an old-fashioned keyhole. The lock held in place a chain that was also brightly polished, made of huge links, obviously well cared for and intended to keep anyone from going through the door. The door itself was old, battered, dark wood, gray with age. The ends and edges of each plank were beaten and ragged.

At the time I thought this must be the archetypal door, the most ancient of all doors. Yet the chain and lock were shiny and unscratched. The door floated before my eyes, about ten or twelve feet away. Suffice it to say I have never seen such a door, in this lifetime at least. Delusion or not, the door was as real to me as any object I can touch or see.

Feel free to speculate on the nature of my vision. Its meaning is so deeply personal I cannot even find words to explain it. If you have had a vision, you will have recognized it as a threshold and very likely understand my strong interest in all kinds of doors and latches and locks to this day.

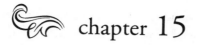

chapter 15

Lucid Dreams

The Chalice

I go to a place. I am looking at a book and I realize we have this book in our bookstore. It is an illustrated children's book about Vikings. I think, "Well, if I'm lucid dreaming, I think I'll choose a page number and look at what's on that page" (all this in the dream). Then I can check later to see if it matches the actual book. I think of a random page number, but I can't read the book and keep getting interrupted.

When I went to the store the next day I recalled the page number, found the book, and looked it up. There was a picture of a chalice. The kicker is that the day before I had the dream, we went to see *The Fisher King*, which was set in modern times but concerned Robin Williams' search for psychological wholeness as he quested after the grail in the form of a chalice. I had looked at the book previous to the dream. I had no specific memory of a chalice, and certainly no conscious recollection of the page number. I sought a direct correspondence of the dream to a material book, and instead happened upon a curiously affirmative coincidence of number, symbol, and experience to my waking life.

The Chase

Over a period of time I have the same dream:

I am being chased by a gang of bad guys. It is night and I am alone. They chase me into a blind alley, from which I am sure I cannot escape.

I always awake just as they are about to catch me, gasping for breath and perspiring. I am frightened until I get a sense of where I am. After a few times, I am aware in the dream that I have had the dream before, but still afraid of being caught.

Finally one night I am having the same dream:

I am being chased and I "know" I will end up in that same blind alley. I decide I am tired of this and I turn to confront the gang. I shout, "What do you want?!" They fall all over themselves to say they are only trying to help me, to get my attention. They have been chasing me because I wouldn't wait for them to catch up to me. They seem as exhausted with the chase as I have been. Then they launch into all the ways that a big strong gang like them can help me. I listen and begin to see their point.

Since that time I have had many dreams in which there is a group of boys or men, and they are always there to help me. They are sometimes accountants, sometimes lawyers, sometimes outlaws, but they are always there to provide helpful information.

It is odd that many of these dreams are black and white, whereas I generally dream in color. At first I thought those chase dreams all occurred at night, but it may be that they seemed dark only because they were not in color. I suspect that all my black-and-white dreams offer messages to me. [This would not be true for every dreamer. Many people only have black-and-white dreams, and color would signal an important dream.]

Lucid dreams occur when you awaken within the dream or become conscious that you are dreaming. Although some control within the dream may follow this revelation, for novices it may be best to ask questions rather than make demands. It is ultimately a greater prize to learn how to repeat and maintain the lucid state than to merely exploit it. To attempt to force a particular experience or reduce the dream state to mere wish fulfillment will generally fail.

One of the most useful potentials of lucidity is for nightmares. It can act as a parachute and allow you to wake from the dream and declare or demonstrate the unreality of a negative experience, or ask a character or a guide in the dream about its underlying meaning. Sometimes it is best to escape a bad dream, sometimes to confront it. Transcending the passivity of the watcher or an unknowing actor within a dream does not mean dreams become less real (unless it is a temporary antidote)—it should make them more real. Lucidity represents omnipotence for your dream consciousness. It is one of the prerequisites to becoming more conscious because it unites your various levels of consciousness within the dream.

Dreams are creative projects between the dreamer and the subconscious. They are part of your reality, the internal communication of your senses. They are no less real than any other experience. They are merely less corporeal. Knowing this, and in particular knowing it as you dream, allows your dream worlds to evolve, become less fragmented and random and develop themselves into episodes of a journey toward self-awareness.

You may be able to change the action in a lucid dream. In most dreams you are an observer of or participant in the drama, but in some dreams you can make decisions to change the action. Many people find that as they listen by recording and analyzing their dreams, they begin to have control over the dreams themselves. For them, no other effort is needed to gain control than merely paying attention. Others find that detailed recording and analysis of dream contents tends to cause them to awaken before a dream is complete. This may stop the dream before lucidity can begin. If this happens, try jotting down only the main characters, events, or feelings of a dream for a while. Then you may be able to quickly fall asleep again and re-enter the dream.

How can you tell when you are about to begin lucid dreaming? What dream events precede a lucid dream? Some people find that they begin to float or fly. Another element is the ability to see yourself in a mirror, or to see parts of your own body. There may be tunnels, snow falling, redheads, dancing, music-making, or white light. Whatever the trigger, you realize that you are dreaming while you are still in the dream. Then you are able to shape the scene, the action, and even the characters in the dream.

Many people are able to program the content of their dreams before going to sleep, but they are not able to affect the dream while they are in it. Lucid dreaming implies only awareness of the dream as it is unfolding. Affecting the dream is not necessary to its definition. In fact, in the first example above there is awareness of the dream state before the page selection occurred. Sometimes the reverse occurs, and a bold action results in awareness of power, which in turn triggers lucidity. The decision to confront the gang in the second dream reflects awareness of the dream state.

Note that this conscious attitude in the dream is different from the simple recurring dream, in which the dream action is replayed until it becomes familiar, thereby relieving the anxiety it once caused. What was first perceived to be a nightmare may, on its own, become simply a not-very-pleasant dream. Facing fears in your dreams generally builds emotional strength. Of course it is not good to just stick your tongue out at dream monsters and say, "Na-na-na-na-na. What can you do to me anyway?" This kind of challenge implies that the dream monster is frivolous when in fact he has value.

You will probably find that lucid dream segments are scattered among other dreams, or that there are lucid moments within a dream. It is useful to continue to experience a variety of dreams and not force them to become lucid. All dreams have some value.

chapter 16

Anxiety Dreams

During periods of great stress, you may find that you have a series of dreams, not necessarily repetitive, in which you are in difficult situations. You feel, in the dream, that you cannot resolve the problem. You may be running to or from something, or you may be taking a test, like in high school or college. You may be on the freeway in your car and unable to get to an exit. Such dreams all incorporate the anxious feeling that you won't perform well.

Usually these dreams reflect the waking condition of your life. They are a message from your unconscious mind that you are under pressure. While the dreams reflect your waking reality, they may include elements that suggest solutions to the waking problems. For example, if you are running in the dreams, you might consider getting up a few minutes early in the morning, or taking a few minutes before supper, and running (or walking) around the block. The physical exercise will release the tension in your body, and you may find you sleep more soundly.

If you are faced with impossible test questions in your dreams, you may want to consider what had challenged you during your day and write a question for your dream to answer. The more specific your question, the more helpful your dream can be. For instance, you may have spent the day working on your tax return. You can't seem to get all the information together to get a refund. You may formulate a question like, "I know I am missing an important piece of information for my tax return. Please give me a picture of it." The next morning, record your dream(s), and look for the answer to the question.

Even if the dreams seem unrelated, look for an answer anyway. You may be surprised how helpful this can be. The dreams may answer the question directly, or they may indicate that you have been unnecessarily worried. For instance, one dream may show you completing the forms and sending the tax return, then taking a break with some friends.

This would suggest that tax return anxiety is a common thing, something to be gotten through, but not a major life crisis.

On the other hand, one dream may suggest that your worry is appropriate to the situation. You may have another anxious dream, but in the middle of it a commentator says, "Yes, I see you are running away from those fellows chasing you, and well you should. They are not there to help you." Awake, you may realize that some of your acquaintances have been pushing you to do something that is not in your best interest, or you may see that you need to change jobs in order to be among like-minded individuals. If instead the commentator says, "Why don't you ask those fellows what they want?" and if you can act on this suggestion, the dream can turn around completely and offer the opportunity to begin lucid dreaming.

You may find that simply accepting an anxious dream is enough to relieve the pressure. You feel that the unconscious process is reflective of, and therefore supportive of, your waking state. Remember that anxiety occurs when you fear the outcome of an unresolved situation. Generally, as you reach conscious resolution, the anxiety recedes. Even when you can't resolve the problem, attention to your dreams can bring relief by showing you that your inner self sees the problem and is sympathetic about it.

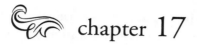 chapter 17

Nightmares

The Ghost

I am in my house, but I am alone. I have intense fear and dread of the upstairs, which is a finished attic. I feel there is a ghost that lives up there and that if I go past the storage closet at the top of the stairs, it will chase me and get me. This ghost is omniscient— it knows I am thinking about it and comes to get me. I run through the house to escape. I try to scream but no sound comes out. I fumble with the key to the back door, and finally get out of the house, but the ghost chases me around the house as well. I awake before the ghost catches me.

I had this dream many times, beginning in fifth or sixth grade. When I was fourteen the dream changed:

I am downstairs, avoiding the attic, and trying not to think of the ghost. I begin to panic and search for the back door. I get out and am running and trying to scream. Then I stop in my tracks. It occurs to me that I have never seen this ghost and I probably have nothing to be afraid of. I go back in the house and look for the ghost. I look everywhere and cannot find her. Then I check a second time in the attic and I find her in the storage closet. I open the door and see a ghostly white woman in a flowing white dress, like an animated black-and-white photo. I walk toward her and I speak. She approaches me and wraps her arms around me in an embrace. I feel a strong sense of friendship with her. I turn around and leave the room.

I awoke and knew I would never have that nightmare again.

Most people can at least recall having nightmares, if not the specific content of those dreams. In the *Jungian-Senoi Dreamwork Manual,* the author defines a nightmare as "any dream from which we wake ourselves up in fear" (Williams 1980, 197). This very simple definition suits most of the nightmares I have heard from clients. Several of the dream examples presented in earlier chapters could then be classified as nightmares: Nebuchadnezzar surely was frightened by his dream; being pulled under the water by some animated vine is a nightmare image. An elephant on the porch would scare most of us, as would being chased by a gang of thugs or getting caught by a ghost. All of these scenarios are enough to leave us scared witless.

The nightmare calls upon us to face something in the dream state that we are not facing in the waking state. It provides us with the golden opportunity to develop strengths within the psyche and deal with forces outside ourselves in our waking life. Often it is not possible to know what is the relationship between waking and dreaming life. The nightmare makes no sense to us, except that it causes great fear.

Three possible actions are possible when nightmares occur:

1. You can simply accept the nightmare and take no conscious action. This may lead to repetition of the dream, with no resolution.

2. You can take action within the dream. When you confront the fearsome dream image or action, you resolve it. Generally when you do this, the dream image will convert into a helper of some kind, or you fight the battle and win, or you stay in the dream to see the ending.

3. You can take action in your waking life. For example, you can return to the dream via active imagination, either alone or with the help of a therapist or other guide. You can play-act a confrontation. If you don't like the first result, you can reset the stage and try, again and again, until you have a satisfactory resolution of the nightmare. This activity examines the details of the dream and changes them to permit a different feeling or outcome.

Nightmares, like all dreams, are extremely personal. You may tell other people about them and they won't fully understand. What causes you tremendous fear may be a nearly ordinary experience for others, or you may not be able to convey the profound sense of dread you felt in the dream. Other people may try to talk you out of the fear, without understanding its source at all. You may have to work with the dream for years in order to understand it, and even then you may never grasp it completely. The nightmare may contain a non-personal archetype of a very bad thing. The best we can do with this is to acknowledge that bad things happen, and are a part of life.

The willingness to face a nightmare, or any other dream, is an act of courage. You only make personal progress when you can face the fear of change. You only make spiritual progress toward self-realization when you face the inner demons as well as the outer ones. This willingness to act in the face of profound fear is courage—going to the heart (*coeur* in French) of the matter with your whole heart. It involves the capacity of mental and moral strength to act. As you develop the ability to stay with difficult dream images and work out their meanings, you develop the ability to persevere through difficult times in your social affairs. Courage does not mean you are no longer afraid—it means you are able to face the fear and deal with it.

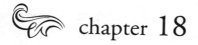

chapter 18

Erotic Dreams

The Drunken Man

A drunken Swedish man comes into a village house where I am visiting. He speaks English. He makes suggestive remarks about using the pump. He assures me that he does know how to use it. I scream and run away from him. I get away, and look for people to help me.

The Girl with the Penis

I see a female child about six or eight years old. She is naked. She is clearly a girl, but has a penis that is adult size. It is fully erect, and circumcised. She also has a white crocheted bikini, feminine looking, but the shape of a man's bikini. She puts it on and I see it is a bit loose. We can see the penis through the crocheted fabric. I ask her what she thinks about being a girl and also having a penis. She says it is okay, but strange to see it through the bikini. I notice that she does not seem to have testicles, but does have a vagina.

Sex with Two Men

I am with two men that I know, and I am attracted to both of them. One seems distant, and I agree to have sex with the other. We are in bed when the distant one comes into the room. I shrug my shoulders and say, "Now what do I do?" I don't have sex with the second man. We get up and he leaves.

Then I am in the living room with the distant one, on the couch, kissing. My grandmother is there. I tell the man we should go where she cannot see us because she won't like what we are doing. It is nearly dawn. I say something about not getting any sleep, but we go ahead with our kissing. There is no actual intercourse in the dream.

Awake, I feel rested, and the headache of the day before is completely gone.

Sigmund Freud, in his study of dreams and dream symbols, suggests that all dreams constitute wish fulfillment of some kind and that for adults the content is primarily sexual. Any dream content according to Freud, therefore, is to be interpreted as sexual. Any violence in a dream is essentially rape, and certainly any shooting, stabbing, or even a key in a lock is to be interpreted as sexual intercourse.

To Freud, all objects belong to one of two categories: the masculine or the feminine group. The group is defined by shape and use. In the first dream above, for example, the reference to the pump would be interpreted as penis envy. Such a definition is extremely limiting in dream interpretation. In a remote village, the pump reference would be a totally appropriate way to get instruction about how to draw water from a well, and the dream might continue with other lessons about living in the country.

According to traditional interpretation, any dream symbol could have an indirect meaning and could be a sign of foretelling. Freud's own Jewish heritage suggests a broader interpretation of dreams and their symbols. "The Talmud has discovered the interesting method of interpreting sexual dreams not always as immediately meaningful but often as indirectly significant or portentous" (Cirlot 1971, xlvii).

Carl Jung disagreed with Freud. While he said that some dreams are about wish fulfillment, many of them express a dissatisfaction with waking life. Many are metaphorical expressions. For example, water flowing from a tap could represent ejaculation, but by the same token, ejaculation could represent a burst of creative energy of any sort. "Psychologically speaking the *membrum* [penis] is itself . . . an emblem of something whose wider content is not at all easy to determine. But primitive people, who, like the ancients, make the freest use of phallic symbols, would never dream of confusing the phallus, as a ritualistic symbol, with the penis. The phallus always means the creative *mana,* the power of healing and fertility, the 'extraordinarily potent,' whose equivalents in mythology and in dreams are the bull, the ass, the pomegranate, the *yoni,* the he-goat, the lightning, the horse's hoof, the dance, the magical cohabitation in the furrow, and the menstrual fluid, to mention only a few of the thousand other analogies" (Jung 1974, 105).

The second dream above focuses the dreamer's attention on the possibility of having both male and female genitalia (albeit incomplete). The dreamer could be either male or female. The erotic feeling of seeing both together could be a metaphor for intercourse, but it very likely has the deeper meaning of a desire for completeness within the self and may signal movement in that direction. The child in the dream may suggest the curiosity or wonder of discovering something new and different. Thus the sexual component catches the attention, provides erotic arousal, and allows for psychological integration of masculine and feminine components to occur. If you don't find this dream particularly erotic, that is natural. Our own erotic dreams are quite stimulating, while other people's dreams may not arouse us much at all.

Erotic dreams contain some of the most provocative images we can experience. They can affect all the senses, depending on the content, and they can evoke deep feelings of sexual arousal, fear, love, and pain. The ecstatic quality of such dream encounters can exceed any waking sexual experience. When you wake from such a dream, you can often feel physically and emotionally disoriented. And you may feel embarrassed or ashamed.

Sexual activity occupies our thoughts from time to time, but for most of us, the vast majority of our time is taken up with other thoughts and activities. The confusion of phallic symbols with immoral acts has led to repression of thoughts and feelings that might have otherwise led toward psychic wholeness if allowed to develop on their own. Especially in erotic dreams, our conscious moral constructs can limit our capacity to learn about our creative urges. If we see only forbidden sexual acts and a fear of rape, we never discover our full creative power and its ecstatic potential.

Modern dream analysts see forthright sexual content of dreams as just that. A phallus in a dream is the equivalent of a life impulse, regardless of whether that impulse is directly sexual in nature or not. A vagina or womb in a dream represents the potential to bear life (a physical child), an idea (a "brain child"), or a spiritual impulse.

According to Jung, sexual union of the masculine and feminine in dreams "is a kind of self-fertilization, a characteristic always ascribed to the mercurial dragon" (1974, 235). The third dream above illustrates this point. There is a shyness or embarrassment (Grandma won't like it). There is interest in two potential sexual partners. But the main thing is the dreamer's rested feeling upon awakening. The dream somehow had provided an experience that relieved the tension of the previous day and allowed the dreamer to awake refreshed. Resolution of a mental or emotional dilemma had apparently occurred.

When an erotic dream contains frightening sexual partners or forceful acts, it is important to consider the possibility that your inner being has been trying to get your attention in subtle ways and, unsuccessful, has resorted to images and feelings that will get your attention. Here, as in other kinds of dreams, the unconscious dream mind has little or no capacity to moderate its impact. Thus a simple sexual metaphor, such as the penetration of a flower by a hummingbird's bill, can quickly escalate to rape by a demon.

Aside from sex, phallic symbols deal with the nature of penetration in a much broader sense. To penetrate means to discern deeply and acutely. Thus a patently sexual dream may also contain an invitation to look deeper into the dream's content for valuable knowledge emerging from the less conscious part of your psyche. Your dream may reflect your discernment of a question in your waking life. *Depth of penetration* is a marketing term that describes the extent to which a commercial product sells in a particular market. Do you have something to sell to the world? Have you been concerned about how to get it out there to your buying public?

Most phallic symbols have personal meaning beyond their shape. Your insight into their meaning is unique to you. It may share a common meaning with others, but you determine its importance. Where Freud would have said that a pencil moving across a sheet of white linen paper is clearly an image of blackening the purity of your female lover (or that your own purity is being smudged, if you are female), we can also find at least three alternative interpretations:

1. You are a writer, and this dream is about you writing something important enough to use fresh white paper.
2. You are an artist, and the dream is about you creating a work of art.
3. You need to contact someone you know to tell them something important.

We could go on and on with possibilities. It is evident that the pencil is *not* merely a sexual implement, and it may not have a sexual component at all.

Erotic dream activity offers the opportunity to penetrate the ego complex and pass through to the personal or collective unconscious. Dream symbols relating to penetration, then, show *when* and *how* unconscious insight is revealed, and the content of the insight shows *what* is being offered to you. Feminine symbols reflect that which is penetrated, comprehended, and intuited.

Erotic dream analysis, if it can get past any moral barriers posed by the conscious mind, can assist in our spiritual development, allow us to observe the process of penetrating deeper insight, and help us identify personally meaningful signposts on the path to individuation. Your sexual dream symbols may be virtually meaningless in the context of your waking sex life, and they may mean everything to your psychic development. This is why you must consider your own dreams in the context of your own life and your own developmental path.

In all dream work, and especially with emotionally charged erotic dreams, we need to learn how to suspend judgment of the dream. We need to get our preconceptions about how things ought to be in our moral universes out of the way and look at the dream as a message from an inner source that is not limited by the same moral restrictions. Carl Jung said it this way: "We must renounce all preconceived opinions, however knowing they make us feel, and try to discover what things mean for the patient" (1974, 105). Think of yourself as your own physician. Suspend your judgment when you examine your dreams, and try to discover what your inner being is saying about your deepest source of creative energy.

Having said all that, I also wish to say that you should get all the physical, emotional, and spiritual pleasure from your erotic dreams that you possibly can manage. No one can supply you with the exact images, tastes, sounds, and physical stimulation as well as your dreams can. When you dream you need not experience shyness or fear or shame, although these may be represented in your dreams from time to time. As you work with erotic dreams, you may find that they become even more ecstatic—you learn what you truly want and need. You may find that they issue in a new cycle of creative effort in your waking life that apparently has nothing to do with the dreams themselves. Dream work serves to open you to all the possibilities of the mind, and as we know, erotic possibilities are an important part of human experience.

Because symbols are constantly changing and evolving within an individual's consciousness, they make an impression on your mind and then may sink back into your memory or unconscious. Following your erotic dreams can reveal one series of symbols and how they change over time. Later you may find the same symbol in another kind of dream and relate back to an earlier creative time in your life. Weaving associations to erotic symbols into your waking life thus enriches all experience.

Conclusion

Dreams Are a Part of You

Many dream therapists believe that every dream element is a part of you, and would encourage you to examine your dreams in this way. To show how this may be helpful, let us consider some of the dreams you have read about in this book. In addition to other interpretations, this step helps integrate the dream into your awareness.

My hair is much longer. This is clearly a part of the dreamer, and indicates a message from the inner self.

I am floating in clear water. While it would be difficult to convince a small child that water in a ditch is part of her, it is an obvious symbol of the unconscious, and thus is an integral part of her psyche.

An elephant comes and knocks on the doors and windows. Often in dreams a house is symbolic of the whole being. There is a temptation to think of the elephant as being outside the psyche, but it may be useful to consider what part of the dreamer he is. For example, he is loud, big, and powerful, all qualities the dreamer may have or desire.

I have a baby but I can't find it. This dreamer may ask herself what part of her the baby represents. Is it a fledgling sense of independence that she has some days, and not others? This dream occurs inside a house—inside her psyche. Thus the baby, being in the house, is logically a part of her.

Thousands of pieces of candy in pretty colored wrappers fall from the sky. In this dream there is a piñata that gets broken, but the dreamer can "own" the candy as part of her sweet vision of herself.

. . . my buddy Rocko. The friend often symbolizes a familiar part of the self with whom we are comfortable.

I find two rooms I didn't know I had. This is a great one to own. There is space within the psyche for new and exciting adventures, if we are able to clean up old business.

I saw a tree of great height . . . reaching with its top to the sky . . . it yielded food for all. Nebuchadnezzar's tree is symbolic of himself in his greatest strength and power. Reaching to the sky can be interpreted as hubris—challenging God in his strength. Daniel interprets the dream as being the king.

I see a large spider-like creature . . . The spider may be interpreted as a part of the dreamer, and all archetypal symbolism aside, only the dreamer can decide what it means.

I become aware of a third presence in the room . . . The dreamer is aware of the lover (perhaps the *anima* or *animus*—we don't know the sex of the dreamer). The third presence is yet another part of the personality.

My dead sister is leaning over my bed . . . Here we have a spirit returning to sound the alarm for an infant who is struggling. An alternative interpretation suggests that the mother's own intuition is calling her to action.

Then the Indian came and shook my hand. The American Indian is identified as a spirit guide after the dream series occurred. He can also be interpreted as a "Native American" part of the dreamer herself, perhaps a past life lineage.

I need to find JFK Jr. This is a dream that is certainly an astral dream. Yet we can ask what part of the dreamer can be portrayed as this famous individual? Her courage, perhaps? Or her fears in a new situation?

I remembered to have seen that exact scene in some dream of long [ago]. Shelley's déjà vu experience concerning a dream scene is a psychic one. At the same time the scene, which he said kindled lawless thought, may be a depiction of a corner of his psyche where one does not always follow the conventional rules. It illustrates the eeriness of bumping into Mind beyond Time, the super-awareness part of the self.

I am being chased by a gang of bad guys. This gang represents a helpful part of the psyche. Many women find that the animus appears in dreams as a group of men (the anima is almost always one particularly alluring woman in a man's dream). In the dream the gang turns out to be helpful. Generally, no matter how frightening a dream is, the elements of the dream can be viewed as a helpful message or part of the psyche.

I fear there is an [omniscient] ghost living in the attic storage room. This nightmare of a ghost that will eat the dreamer is wonderful! The dreamer, a very creative, artistic person, fears the omniscient ghost in the attic—the intellect, by most dream working standards. The attic could also be the same supermind as in Shelley's dream—self-knowledge separated from ego. At the age of fourteen the dreamer discovers that her intellect is not something she must fear, but is a powerful, comfortable part of herself. The integration of this ghost shows that the dreamer has taken a giant step on the path to self-awareness.

The more of yourself you bring to the examination of your dreams, the greater the eventual reward as you develop the courage and wisdom to face your inner development as well as your social responsibilities. You also develop the capacity to stay with a problem instead of running away. You experience the joy of discovering yourself and the world. The content of your dreams is at least as vast as your waking life. It provides a frontier of exploration—an interior world only you can investigate. Whether you use the book or the program to explore your dreams, you have the materials at hand to begin the journey of a lifetime. *Bon voyage!*

Part II

Dream Symbol Dictionary

Symbol Dictionary

A

ABANDONMENT

Abandonment in a dream takes on symbolic value in addition to its obvious reflection of a potential reality in waking life. Abandonment by God was one of the acts that revealed Jesus' humanity. Abandonment in a dream is an inability to find yourself, or a part of yourself that is essential to solving whatever problem is presented in the dream. When such an image or feeling appears in a dream, it is a certain indicator that you are searching for something important in your life; it also means that your unconscious mind is aware of the search and is available to help you.

ABNORMALITY

When something abnormal appears in a dream, it is symbolizing the upside-downness of the dream situation. A maimed or abnormally large or small hand, for example, draws attention to that part of the body and suggests that you need to pay attention to it or what it is capable of doing. A large hand may suggest conscious awareness of greater power or force, while a damaged hand may indicate you are feeling protective of it. Also, the abnormal object may have personal meaning to you, and therefore acts to focus your attention.

ABYSS (VOID) (*see also* EMPTINESS, MACROCOSM, NOTHINGNESS, SPACE)

The abyss, or the edge of it, is a frequent dream image. Falling or the fear of falling relates to the diminishment of stature—you feel inferior by reason of being "at the bottom." On the other hand, the abyss suggests the depth of potential and symbolizes the vast possibilities that lie in the unconscious. The Void, or empty space, is also from where a new idea can emerge. Thus a dream of the Void may suggest a creative moment is at hand and serves to prepare a psychic space for the creative process.

ACCIDENT (*see* FALL)

ACHILLES (*see* BALDUR)

ACROBAT

The upside-down or unusual position of the acrobat suggests two extremes. First, you may be "off balance" in your waking life and need the acrobat's skills to regain equilibrium. Second, if you acknowledge the acrobat as part of yourself, your dream is suggesting you have the skills necessary to deal with whatever life hands you. Thus the acrobat appears because you need skills that you may not be consciously aware of but that exist within you already.

ACTIVITY

The action of a dream can be viewed as a dramatic play divided into acts and scenes and populated with actors and props. Every prop, player, and action is significant and may be examined in detail. It is, however, the dreamer's decision what the personal significance may be. You may understand one part of a dream now, and discover added meaning much later.

ADAM

The first man in a dream symbolizes your emerging awareness of yourself as an individual. You are, after all, the first (and only) you. It also points to your connection to those who have gone before you and to the power of the universe that is concentrated in the collective (Adam being older, larger, and more powerful in some respect).

AGE

Often in dreams the age of a person or animal indicates its relative freshness. A newborn is a symbol of something brand new in your thoughts or feelings. A mature cat symbolizes more mature instinct, while an old lion might represent the power needed for leadership—something you don't obtain in a short time. An old lion also represents something about yourself—strength, perhaps, that you are just becoming aware of.

AGREEMENT (CONCORD)

Any agreement in a dream signals a moment when you have resolved a conflict or problem you have been working on. It means that the unconscious is in agreement with the conscious on some point that previously had been unresolved.

AGRICULTURE

Anything growing in a dream is fertile, creative, and therefore enriching. The cultivation of creative ideas is suggested by the dream image. The nature of the crop is significant: if you dream of beets, consider the personal significance of beets, their size, shape, taste, and color. A dream about wheat will have a very different meaning from beets, but will share the metaphor for growth.

AIR

Air in a dream could be just the normal stuff that fills the space around us. It could also symbolize thought, logic, and objectivity. Just as the eagle soars high above and looks down to spy its prey, we mentally find an objective viewpoint from which we can understand more clearly. Flying in dreams often indicates the lucid realm—you have more control over the plot of the dream drama in lucid dreams.

ALCHEMY

We think of alchemy as the process of turning lead into gold. However, it is also symbolic of the inner psychic process of turning the unrefined material of the self into a purer substance. The basic processes involved are solidifying, liquifying, burning, and sublimating, or turning into air. The solidifying process is grounding and earthy and indicates gaining a firmer understanding of something. The liquifying process is watery and dissolving and suggests dipping below the surface of the water (the consciousness) to find what is hidden below (in the feeling or unconscious part of the mind). Burning (or heating) is the creative process of changing the make-up of something (like turning dough into bread or clay into pottery). Sublimating (or turning into air) refers to getting above a situation in order to see the overall picture and thereby gain objectivity. The alchemical model can be used to evaluate all dream activity. The movement from one state of being to another is where personal understanding can be found, so even though burning doesn't sound fun, it can be a way of purifying or cleansing the self of unpleasant baggage.

ALCOHOL

Alcohol is the product of distillation and is therefore is symbolic of an alchemical process—a change—which has taken place. We drink champagne to celebrate a wedding. Christ's blood is symbolically found in the wine of the Eucharist. Thus drinking alcohol in a dream can indicate a positive transformation. It can also be just what it looks like—a beer, a glass of wine, or a beverage you like.

ALLIGATOR (CROCODILE)

Fierce and vicious, hiding beneath the depths of the water to emerge and strike their victims, both alligator and crocodile indicate powerful forces of destruction. In addition to this power, they have the ability to move easily between land and water. Thus they symbolize your ability to move between the material world of waking life and the watery world of dreams and the unconscious. They further symbolize the capacity and willingness to look into the unconscious to find the deeper meaning of something.

ALPHA

Alpha is the first letter of the Greek alphabet and is thus an indicator of beginnings. We also use "A"s to signify superior scores in school. The "A" marks the earning of a grade, or the end of a course of study, and therefore the movement to something new. The alpha member of a pack is the male or female leader. Alpha and omega are the first and last letters of the Greek alphabet and are often used to symbolize God, who is the beginning and end of all things. Still, an "A" in a dream can indicate the name of a person or thing, just as any initial will do.

ALPHABET (*see* LETTERS)

ALUMINUM

A metal valued for its resistance to oxidation, aluminum is shiny, reflective, and conducts heat. Aluminum symbolizes the capacity to reflect energy coming from sources outside the self, as well as the capacity to absorb that which is valuable. As such it may represent a bit of a paradox as a dream element.

AMBIVALENCE (*see* INVERSION)

ANCHOR

The anchor is an early Christian symbol of salvation. Just as it keeps a ship from drifting, an anchor in your dream may symbolically represent a person, object, or feeling that provides stability for you. Most anchors have a vertical piece and a crosspiece, suggestive of the basic mandala.

ANGELS

An angel may appear in your dream to help you or bring information to light. It may also indicate surrounding awesome and invisible forces that can benefit you. Angels and guides can take many forms, and they are companions that exist on a different level of being. If the angel does not speak in the dream, you may want to actively reconnect with it through writing or imagination to find out what message it offers.

The nine orders in the celestial hierarchy (from highest to lowest) are: *Seraphim*—represent peaceful contemplation and include Gabriel, Metatron, and Kemuel;

Cherubim—a class of angels associated with childhood and innocence; *Thrones*—the angels that carry out justice (Raphael is one); *Dominions*—charged with managing the functioning of the universe. (One of these was said to have transported Enoch to heaven); *Virtues*—the angels associated with encouragement, miracles, and blessings; *Powers*—protectors of the world against demons; *Principalities*—protectors of religions; *Archangels*—messengers carrying divine decrees; *Angels*—these work directly with human beings. According to Christian and Jewish traditions, we all have angels assigned to us, although the number varies from one tradition to another.

ANGER

Anger, like all emotions, can become exaggerated in a dream. Evaluate your level of anger in a dream with this in mind: a slight waking irritation could translate to an angry outburst in a dream, while waking frustration and anger could become volcanoes or nuclear explosions in the dream. Anger in a dream is a signal that your waking life is causing distress in some way. The dream may be pointing to a desire for revenge that you are not conscious of, but that you need to address.

ANIMA

The anima is the feminine component of the male personality. Generally it is the less conscious component of the psyche, as most males are more conscious of their masculine side. Some psychologists suggest that women have an anima as well, and there is disagreement about whether it is a conscious or unconscious component of the female psyche. The anima often appears as a seductive, or at least very attractive, feminine figure.

ANIMUS

The animus is the masculine component of the female personality. Generally it is the less conscious component of the psyche, as most women are more conscious of their feminine side. Some psychologists suggest that men have an animus as well, and there is disagreement about whether it is a conscious or unconscious component of the male psyche. The animus often appears as a group of male figures.

ANIMALS

Generally animals are indicators of the instinctual levels of the mind. Depending on the animal, the instinct itself will differ, and the message will be specific to the particular animal. The kitten is cuteness personified, but implies the power of the full grown animal. The nonhuman psyche consists of instincts and of the unconscious. A lesser-evolved animal in a dream may indicate a primitive instinct, or that the instinct is emerging from a deeper level of the unconscious. Animals also serve as companions or allies, and their nature reveals the nature of the companion.

ANTELOPE

American Indian stories include tales of the antelope who gives itself willingly to feed and clothe the people. Yet the people must take action to kill the antelope. The animal's instinct to survive is thereby given to the humans, and the humans give their prayers and thanks to the antelope. The lesson is to take the action necessary to move forward and the antelope in your dreams signifies the beauty and grace of this action. Just as the antelope taught the people how to change their behavior to survive, the dream symbol tells you that change is appropriate and swift action is possible.

ANTIQUES (OLD THINGS)

When dreams include old things, you are coming into contact with several possibilities: (1) something from your past; (2) an elder or predecessor in symbolic form; (3) something you have been carrying or nurturing for a long time; (4) something weary or worn out; (5) something valuable because of its history. If the antique object is something you recognize, then it has built-in associations to your life, and those are important to consider. If it is unknown to you, then the nature of the object itself provides information and it takes on its own symbolic value. If you frequently dream about antiques from a particular part of the world, or a particular culture, then you may be accessing, through dreams, a past life in which you were familiar with those objects. Tracking such objects through dreams, and also recording waking experiences when you are around the objects, can be a powerful way to remember the past life. The value in such memories is in finding their meaning or rediscovering skills you had then, as well as resolving issues in your present life that make no sense without a past life connection. Many deep psychological issues can be laid to rest when the past life connection is revealed and resolved.

ANTS

Consider the attributes of ants: They are amazingly strong and capable of carrying far more than their own weight. They are industrious; they stick to certain tasks for extended periods of time. They are group oriented and capable of working well together toward a common goal. Ants communicate, although we are not exactly sure how. They are busy, and can engage in what in humans would be called compulsive behavior. They therefore exemplify some of the best and worst of human behaviors. What are the ants doing in your dream? Take clues from their activity.

ANVIL

An anvil is used by a blacksmith as a place to pound out the metal of an implement—it is the shape of a thundercloud building up to a storm. We associate the claps of thunder and the clangs of the blacksmith's hammer with the object itself. It is a solid, massive object and may thus represent a weighty matter in your dream. It can also represent the sound of a hammer falling or of thunder, and also represents the power and force behind both.

APOLLO (*see also* WOLF)

Apollo is the Greek god associated with the sun who drives the sun's chariot across the sky each day. He may stand for the sun, a symbol of wholeness, and he may represent a new understanding of your own psychic wholeness. Other possible meanings include creativity, life, energy, the power of life, and hope. Apollo could appear as a wolf.

APPLE

The apple signifies the totality of the universe. Eating the forbidden apple is therefore symbolic of the desire to have and know everything. When the apple is sliced horizontally through its middle, a fivefold pattern is revealed. This is the pattern of the five elements in Chinese cosmology, or of the four elements and the container of ether in Western alchemical tradition. The fivefold pattern signifies all that is creative and fruitful, and the dimensions of the fivefold division are naturally pleasing to the eye.

AQUARIUS

The Water Bearer is the constellation Aquarius and represents the power of the human intellect. It represents the process through which we attain spiritual understanding. The human part of the constellation relates to the power of intellect, while the water relates to the forces of intuition. Thus the symbol unifies the dual facets of mind, and is therefore a symbol of integration.

ARABESQUE (*see* LABYRINTH)

ARCHANGELS (*see* ANGELS)

ARCHITECTURE (BUILDINGS)

Architecture is the result of human activity. Buildings reflect the human body and human functions in their details. For example, windows parallel eyes and the ability to see beyond one's own body. In addition, the particular type of architecture is significant to the meaning of the dream. The complexity of architectural elements suggests the complexity of even the simplest building in a dream—it symbolically represents the complexity of our physical, mental, emotional, and spiritual existence. Thus buildings suggest that the dream is not as simple as it may appear on the surface—investigation will very likely turn up a hidden significance.

ARIES

Aries is the god of war, but also of agriculture. The sun is in the Aries part of the zodiac in the spring when plants begin to emerge from the earth in the Northern Hemisphere, thus Aries symbolizes of the emergence of life and the pioneering spirit. Aries also relates to the original impulse of any activity. In astrology Aries governs the head and the brain, the supposed source of physical and spiritual energies.

ARK

An ark in a dream represents the capacity to preserve and protect something of value. Its structure is reminiscent of the ego complex, which floats on the surface of the waters of the unconscious, and mediates between the conscious and the unconscious. As such the ego complex provides the capacity for wholeness, and the ark is therefore a symbol of wholeness.

ARM

The arm symbolizes strength, activity, and offerings. What the arm is doing reveals something significant to the dream. The arms of a dream figure may not be significant in and of themselves, but if the word "arm" is in your dream journal, then the arms are probably the focus of action and are therefore more important. The arm represents strength to a certain extent, even though it may be thin or appear weak in the dream.

ARMADILLO

The armadillo is heavily plated with body armor. In your dream it symbolizes the protection you have around you, or it could mean that you need to pay attention and develop some protection. In both cases you are called upon to understand your persona or mask, and then to use that mask well in the world. First you must understand the difference between your true self and the mask you show to others, and the dream symbol may be inviting you to think about the difference.

ARROW

Arrows represent the male component of the psyche—linear thought processes, directed activities, and action taken outside the self. They also symbolize messages and travel—any kind of movement.

ARROYO (see CANYON)

ASCENSION

Anything that ascends or rises up in your dream symbolizes the spiritual value of higher consciousness. The act of ascension is the act of rising above the ordinary. Elevators and stairs that ascend are indicators of a more intellectual or spiritual consideration, as contrasted with descending into the unconscious. However, the unconscious is not a place of lesser value, or less spiritual in its content. Unconscious contents are simply unavailable to the conscious awareness. Psychologically, both actions of descending and ascending arrive at the place of wholeness, and simply provide more than one path to the goal.

Ass (Donkey)

This animal can indicate a couple of things in a dream: First, it can be a symbol for patience and humility as it is a beast of burden. Mary rode a donkey to the place where Jesus was born, and Jesus rode a donkey into Jerusalem to his own trial and death. Thus the donkey can be a messenger of death or transformation, and may appear when you are undergoing major changes in your life. Second, it can be a symbol of wisdom, as it is associated with Saturn, the teacher.

Attic

The attic symbolizes a storehouse of information and memory for you. Going to the attic may symbolize going back into childhood memories to find something important. It is interesting that the attic stores childhood memories, and is also the part of the house closest to the sky which symbolizes spirit and higher aspirations.

Autumn (*see* Fall)

Axes (Sharp) (*see also* Knife, Sword)

All sharp implements are symbolic of power and force and are also human in origin. Thus they symbolize the mind's capacity to cut through confusing or contradictory elements to arrive at a decision. Because these instruments are used to cut or divide things, they also symbolize the duality of experience in the material world.

Babylon

The symbol of Babylon is of something old, something gone from your present life. There is a feeling of beauty, but perhaps also of loss. A focal point will be anything in the dream that does not belong in the setting—a modern telephone or other object, or an idea that is more contemporary.

BACK

When you see the back of a person in a dream, you are focusing on the structure of that person's being. The spine is the body's principal support and even clothed it represents the perceived strength of the individual. Also, you may not be able to recognize the person if his or her back is turned to you, and you may not even be able to identify the person's sex with certainty.

BADGER

The badger is an aggressive, powerful animal that attacks with fierce rage. It digs for food among the roots of plants. The message of these two facts is that you may need to dig into the roots of your anger to understand it. Anger is a useful tool when it is controlled, and the badger shows you that rage is not so useful. Learning to control the energy behind anger can give you the power to attain success. Learn your personal boundary between aggression and meaningful assertiveness.

BALD EAGLE (*see* EAGLE)

BALDNESS

If you know the bald person in the dream, then baldness has no special significance. However, if the person is not naturally bald, or if baldness itself is the most prominent feature of the dream character, then it has greater significance. A lack of hair may symbolize a lack of intellectual power or control. In a male it may indicate a degree of learning that comes with greater age. It could be one way for the dream ego to indicate security is stripped away, similar to being naked in a dream.

BALDUR (ACHILLES)

A Norse god and son of Odin, Baldur was granted protection by all plants except for mistletoe, which was eventually the cause of his death. His story is reminiscent of Achilles who was invulnerable except for his heel where he sustained a mortal wound. The symbol is one of near invulnerability in which the single vulnerable area can be of paramount importance.

BANDAGES

A bandage in a dream can reflect the psychic awareness of an actual injury or weakness. It can symbolize the general feeling of injury, but also of protection from further hurt. Thus it is an element included by the psyche as a sign that things will be all right.

BANK

As a large, secure building, a bank symbolizes the strength and power of the mind filled with valuable thoughts, not the least of which is self-esteem. If you feel you are a stranger in the bank, then you may also feel your self-esteem is subject to someone else's control. A sloping river bank symbolizes access to the unconscious (a deep, watery place). If steep, the access is abrupt and perhaps frightening; if gradual, you feel that entering the unconscious world is relatively easy and safe.

BANNER (*see* FLAG)

BASEMENT (CELLAR)

The basement or cellar symbolizes unconscious territory. We store memories and feelings from the past in the unconscious, and in a dream you may go to the cellar to retrieve them. A descent to a second level below the basement may indicate a search in the collective unconscious for deeper meaning, beyond what you can personally remember. Many dream symbols have a broader collective meaning which is often more important than any personal memory.

BASILISK

This mythological beast is said to have the power to kill all who look at it. In a dream it may symbolize the power within you to take care of yourself, even in extreme situations. Just as the beast protects treasure in stories, in the dream you seem to be protecting yourself, your greatest treasure.

BASKET

A basket may symbolize the material body. In Buddhism, the Three Baskets are the containers of the three aspects of faith: Hinayana, Mahayana, and Vajrayana Buddhism.

BAT

Bats live in caves and come out at night to hunt. They have poor vision and rely on their sense of hearing to find food. Associated with vampires, the bat is symbolic of rebirth, and that rebirth does not have to have any negative connotations. Your dream may be indicating that you need to search through the dark portions of your unconscious to uncover something even more potent than the self. Just as the bat hangs upside down in its cave, your dream suggests that you are undergoing some form of initiation in which your life path reverses or transforms in some way.

BATH

Immersion may symbolize cleanliness in a dream. It can also symbolize the transformation of baptism. A third possibility is the purification of elements in alchemy. The water itself may symbolize the unconscious. Finding yourself in a comfortable bath in a dream probably includes a bit of each of these symbolic meanings.

BATTLE (*see* **WAR**)

BEAR

In alchemy the bear is related to the initial stages of work and thus represents the instinctual level of mind. A bear in your dream may indicate the need to pay attention to your own instincts, instead of mindlessly following others. The bear follows its own wisdom. The bear is related to the goddess Diana, and thus to the moon. Bears hibernate in the winter, so you may be receiving a message to withdraw from some of your activities and rest for a period of time.

BEATING (*see* **FLOGGING**)

BEAVER

The beaver is industrious. It blends water and earth energies together to form a happy home for itself. The beaver may indicate that you are working together with others in harmony to achieve good results. It may indicate the need to get down to the business of the dream. The beaver symbolizes the ability to re-engineer your environment to suit your needs.

BEE (*see also* **FLEUR-DE-LIS**)

Bees have a complex social organization. This symbol appears in royal coats of arms, perhaps recognizing the hierarchical organization of the hive, and perhaps recognizing the industrious creativity of a social system where leadership is key. Diligence is another facet of the bee's behavior. Bees also symbolize fertility, as they carry pollen from one flower to another. The bee in a dream, therefore, presents a complex array of possible meanings, including the capacity to sting the unwary.

BELL (**GONG**)

Bells hold sacred value in many religions. Bells and gongs provide vibrational tones to focus the mind in meditation. It may symbolize a specific feeling or tone important in this dream, or it may reflect a meditative state within the dream.

BELLY (**GUT**)

The intestines are where the assimilation of food occurs, and reflect the assimilation of ideas and feelings from the unconscious into consciousness. This is also where gut reactions are felt, and thus indicate that you can trust your intuitive responses.

BELT (*see also* **BICYCLE**, **MANDALA**)

A belt forms a circle, and all circles participate in the symbolism of mandala.

BICYCLE (*see also* BELT, MANDALA)

The two wheels suggest the two sides of the mind: intellect and intuition. The vehicle moves you forward in the dream; intellect and intuition work together to help you solve problems in your waking life. Wheels are circles, and hence reflect the qualities of mandala.

BIRDS

People have always been fascinated with flight. We think of angels as having wings, and therefore as more elevated spiritually. The dove symbolizes peace and brought the assurance of survival to Noah in the ark. Each bird has its own symbolic meaning, but generally birds in dreams symbolize rising to a higher spiritual level, or receiving aid from a supernatural source.

BISON (BUFFALO)

The buffalo provided everything American Indians needed for survival—food, warm hides for clothing, and more. It is possible to eat very large quantities of buffalo meat at one sitting, as it is apparently very digestible. The powerful attraction of abundance can steer you off the proper spiritual path, so be cautious when this image appears in a dream. It has both the fullness of abundance and the danger of an animal that weighs so much. The white buffalo is sacred to the Lakota and is a bringer of ceremonies.

BITE

To be bitten in a dream may indicate that you are subject to an upsurge of instinctual or unconscious material in your dreams. While you have to take care with sudden floods of unconscious material, this can be a beneficial force in your life. To bite in a dream may indicate that you are aware of your animal instincts and capabilities.

BLACK

The color black is associated with minerals. It is also the color of death and putrefaction, and thus the color of the fertilizer that allows new growth. Black is the color of night. Black-and-white dreams are sometimes mistaken for dreams in nighttime settings. Black is the color of church vestments used for funerals and Good Friday. Black is the color of the Void. It is sometimes thought to reflect the intuitive process. Black is the color of the Shadow, that part of yourself that resides in the unconscious.

BLACK WIDOW

This spider has earned a poisonous reputation, but it is not as dangerous as many people think. Still, it is a potent dream symbol, since it carries on its body an hourglass symbol. It may indicate that the time has come for you to make changes—and that any change will serve you at this point in time, even one that seems negative. Sometimes any movement is preferable to stagnation.

BLACKBIRD

A blackbird symbolizes the Shadow, the unconscious darker side of our nature. A blackbird also indicates that magic is afoot. It can be an omen of things to come, so listen to what it has to say. You may want to go back into the dream and ask it to tell you its message if it didn't speak in the dream.

BLACKSMITH

The blacksmith symbolizes the capacity to make something useful out of dull materials. The smith takes ordinary metal and tempers it in the fire, one of the many alchemical and psychological processes of seeking purification of your being. The smith has the strength to endure the heat of the process, and symbolizes your inner strength.

BLOND-HAIRED PERSON

Light hair is associated with the air element, and therefore with thoughts and ideas. In a dream a blond-haired, or fair person, can symbolize the quality of fairness.

BLOOD

In Christianity Jesus offered his blood for the salvation of souls. In a dream, blood can be the logical outcome of an injury, or it can symbolize your willingness to take action in the face of danger—the willingness or capacity to sacrifice.

BLOUSE (*see* CLOTHES, SHIRT)

BLOWING (*see* BREATH)

BLUE

Blue reflects thinking and the alchemical process of rising up to achieve objectivity. Blue is also the color of the throat chakra. Sometimes it symbolizes devotion and religious values (the color of Mary's robes). In Buddhism blue is the color of clarity of mind—mirror-like wisdom. It is the color of transition between water and air, and like the blue water of a calm lake which reflects the blue of the sky. Blue may represent feelings of sadness or depression in a dream, or the most transcendent part of your being.

BLUE JAY

Blue jays are loud, raucous, irritating birds. As small as they are, they have the power to attract attention, and in your dream they may be calling attention to something you may have overlooked. Blue, which is the color of the sky, can be associated with thinking, and more specifically with objective thought. According to Sun Bear (1994, 149), the blue jay begins life as a black bird and changes to blue. This parallels the transformation of the dark *prima materia* to the *lapis,* or purified essence.

BLUEBIRD

The bluebird is associated with happiness. Paradoxically it is also associated with sadness. The sky appears blue from the ground, and the earth appears blue from space. The Virgin Mary's purity is symbolized by her blue robe. The bluebird may be an indication that you are being purified, and that apparent paradoxes in your life will soon be resolved.

BOAR (see HOG, PIG)

BOAT

Any vessel in the water can be seen as the ego—the connection between the intellect (air) and the unconscious (water). While the boat remains on the surface, it can be viewed as a vehicle that travels between conscious and unconscious realms. A sinking boat suggests an unforeseen or perilous descent into the unconscious.

BOBBIN (see SPINDLE)

BOBCAT

This wild creature looks as cute as a housecat but is ferocious and potentially dangerous. It is a solitary animal and shares in the power symbolized by all cats. The bobcat sees and hears very well, and may be suggesting that you pay attention to both in your daily life.

BODY (see also CURL, HAIR, HEAD)

The body is the container for the mind, soul, and spirit. The condition of a body in a dream can be seen as an indicator of your own self-esteem or psychological state. The body doesn't have to be yours. If it belongs to someone you know, it could make you aware of a trait you share with that individual.

BOG (see MARSH)

BOLT (FASTENER, LATCH, LOCK, SCREW)

A lock or latch symbolizes the capacity to protect your inner being from outside influence, or to protect your conscious mind from invasion of unconscious material that could be too difficult to experience. Any fastener symbolizes the desire to attach one thing to another, or to keep two things attached to each other. The latch or screw may take the place of the desire to flee in the dream.

BONE (see also SKELETON)

Bones represent a structure of things that is difficult to destroy. They are hard on the outside and have softer marrow inside. The "bare bones" are the simple facts, unadorned with embellishments. Perhaps the dream is offering the simple truth about a problem you are working on.

BONSAI TREE (*see* **ESPALIER**)

BOOK

Generally books symbolize the record of something. They can provide that record to inform you, or they can symbolize the fact that records exist. To "make book" is to place a bet on a sure thing. To "book a reservation" is to record that you plan to take action at some time in the future.

BOTTLE

Bottles generally contain edible substances, and in a dream they can symbolize something valuable to you indirectly. Genies are kept in bottles, and the genie is a very creative being. All sorts of elixirs come in bottles, and they might represent your own talents that you keep bottled up inside. Messages in bottles are set afloat with the hope that someone will eventually read them, and thus the bottle contains information instead of an actual drink.

BOW (CURTSY, TIE)

The bow represents power, as it is used to shoot arrows longer distances than you can reach with your arms. The bow, when flexed, contains a tension that can be useful. There is an American Indian legend about a boy who wants to visit his father, the sun, and he becomes an arrow and is shot all the way up to the sun—a story about the great power of intention. A bow tie is one that can be undone very easily. It protects the throat, and therefore the throat chakra. It is an item of formal attire, and may thus represent the need for formal speech. If it is not formal, then the dream image is one of more casual, relaxed speech. To curtsy or bow in a dream is to acknowledge something that is either greater than yourself or that deserves your respect. If dream characters bow to you, the dream message is that you are worthy of respect. The bow is the part of the ship that cuts through the water. Standing in ship's bow in a dream is symbolic of forging ahead into the unknown territory of the unconscious mind, or of forging ahead in your waking life into the unknown future.

BOX

All receptacles symbolize the feminine, the hidden, and the unconscious. None of these are inherently destructive, but they all have hidden aspects that evoke curiosity and sometimes dread. Pandora certainly found the contents of her box to be a mixed blessing. However, you will never know what your dream box contains until you open it. Sparring, or boxing, in the ring symbolizes the struggle to deal with the contents of your mind and the events in your daily life. The more vigorous the fight, the more difficult your problem. Still, you are in the ring because you know both how to protect yourself and how to forge ahead.

BRAIDS (PLAIT) (*see also* CADUCEUS, CHAIN)

Braids represent threads of a story or of a problem that are woven together into a whole. What factors in your waking life do you feel are involved with the braid? Braids are stronger than single strands of hair or fibers in a rope. Ideas or feelings associated with the braid hold together firmly and will support other ideas.

BRAMBLE (THICKET)

Just as brambles grew up in the fairy tale to prevent the prince from finding Sleeping Beauty, a bramble or thicket represents a prickly maze to be navigated in order to achieve a goal. In the fairy tale the thorns keep the prince out. In the story of Brer Rabbit, the thorns provide protection for the rabbit from his enemy, the fox. Thus brambles can represent either a barrier or protection.

BRANCH

Tree branches are often used to symbolize the members of your family. They also mimic the veins and arteries in the human body. Branches can indicate you are reaching for greater objectivity in the dream. The branches of a river flow together. This is a m etaphor for taking different ideas and merging them into one. You may be searching for a solution to a problem and by letting energies flow naturally you will see the possibility of synthesis. The branches of your family, appearing in a dream, can remind you of the diversity of your heritage. These individuals can also represent parts of yourself that are different and yet part of the whole.

BRAND (MARK)

Brands establish the identity of the owner or creator of something. In your dream they may symbolize unconscious content that you can own in consciousness.

BRASS

Because brass can be polished as bright as gold but has less monetary value, it may symbolize the brightness of personality without the spiritual depth gold represents. The blend of metals in brass is very useful in making everyday tools. Brass is associated with the planet Venus because one of the metals in it is copper (the other metal in this alloy is zinc, which is associated with Jupiter, Saturn, Uranus, or Pluto by different astrologers). The brassy personality is loud, jarring, strident, sassy, impudent.

BREASTS

The breast is the source of physical nurturance for the infant. For both males and females, the breast also indicates a source of emotional nurturing, and this symbolism carries through into adulthood. Touching and sucking are the earliest forms of contact for the infant, and we never outgrow the desire for significant connections. Even a solitary monk seeks a connection to the physical world and may have erotic dreams.

BREATH (BLOWING)

The breath symbolizes the life force we share with nature. It also symbolizes nourishment of the mind and the self. God breathed life into Adam and Eve, and for Hindus the breath of God represents a long cycle of physical existence. Blowing symbolizes life carried by the wind. Blowing on something, then, symbolizes giving it life. We blow on dandelions and scatter its seed.

BREEZE (CYCLONE, TORNADO, WHIRLPOOL, WHIRLWIND) (*see also* HURRICANE, WIND)

The movement of air is a metaphorical representation of the movement of ideas. A breeze is suggestive of change; a gale is more dramatic. What is the strength and quality of the air movement in the dream? Forceful wind suggests the need for a more energetic examination of your waking situation or the circumstances associated with the dream itself.

BRIDGE

Bridges symbolize the capacity, need, or opportunity to cross from one set of circumstances to another. In many cultures the bridge joins heaven and earth, or two very different worlds of experience. In a dream the bridge is the link between what you consciously can perceive and the less conscious side of your mind. The bridge is symbolic of transition.

BROKEN OBJECTS (*see also* FRACTURE)

Sometimes we must break something open to see the inside. A broken object can indicate an "inside" piece of information you are presented with in the dream. If the object is familiar to you, consider what its deeper meaning or value may be. The dream does not mean that an object that is presently whole will break in the future. It could be an indication that something associated with the object will undergo a change.

BRONZE

Bronze is a combination of metals used for making statues and implements. It maintains a rich henna color when polished, but requires care. Thus in a dream, a bronze object indicates the need for you to care for something to maintain its health and beauty. Bronze is associated with the planet Venus because one of the metals in it is copper (the other main metal in this alloy is tin, with traces of other elements). The use of this metal developed between 4000 and 3000 B.C. In a dream bronze may symbolize something antique and rare.

Brown

Brown is the color of the earth—both the healthy growth potential and the dirty qualities. Brown is solid, grounded. It is the color of the sign Capricorn, and thus indicates ambition in the material world.

Bubbles

Bubbles symbolize the contents of the unconscious or an internal source, and their appearance signals a moment when inner resources are becoming conscious, much the way bubbles rise through water to the surface. They are filled with air, the element associated with objectivity. Thus something you are less aware of enters your conscious thinking.

Buckle

Because buckles fasten your belt around you, or around a piece of luggage, for example, they symbolize the security and protection afforded by the clothing or container. Thus a buckle symbolizes the value of containment.

Buffalo (*see* Bison)

Buildings (*see* Architecture)

Bulk/Bulkiness

Anything bulky is substantial, and thus symbolizes the practical, down-to-earth aspect of your dream. Largeness suggests power.

Bull (Cow) (*see also* Ox)

The bull is associated with the zodiac sign Taurus and is a powerful fertility symbol. It is a symbol of the sun in many cultures. While the cow is thought of as a domesticated animal, the bull has more powerful tendencies toward becoming angry or unruly ("bull in a china shop"). The cow or bull in a dream can point to issues of productivity in your waking life.

Bunch (Cluster)

A bunch or cluster of something—grapes, flowers, and so on—symbolizes the multifaceted nature of something you are working on. This symbol suggests you take a broad view and consider the variety of information being offered, either in the dream or in your waking life. What elements in the dream provide contrasting and supporting information?

Burning (*see* Cremation)

BUTTERFLY

The butterfly symbolizes transformation as it changes from a caterpillar to a butterfly. It is a symbol of the zodiac sign Gemini. In a dream, transformation is often presented in symbolic terms, and the butterfly means transformation into something beautiful and light. As such it is symbolic of the soul, which survives through transformation or rebirth.

C

CADUCEUS (PLAIT) (*see also* BRAIDS, CHAIN)

This symbol of the medical community may mean you can anticipate some contact with a physician in the near future. However, it can also indicate that you have a more fully developed understanding of your own or another person's physical needs. As a type of wand, it symbolizes creativity.

CAGE (*see* ENCLOSURE)

CALENDAR (*see* YEAR)

CAMEL

The camel carries its own water supply and can subsist in the desert for many days. Thus it symbolizes strength and endurance when it appears in a dream. It also symbolizes temperance or sobriety, as it moderates its use of the water it has stored.

CANARY

The canary has a beautiful song and may symbolize the voice in your dream. They are sensitive creatures, and the voice is sensitive to its physical and emotional surroundings.

CANCER

The zodiacal sign of the summer solstice, Cancer symbolizes the capacity to flow with the course of the stream and not fight against it. This implies the ability to perceive where the current is running. In a dream it indicates movement within the unconscious.

CANDLE

The lighted candle is a symbol of individual inspiration, as opposed to unity. The candle is often used to focus the mind in meditation or spell work.

CANOPY

The canopy is a symbol of protection, as in the entrance to a hotel which protects guests from rain or snow. It may also symbolize an elevated position, as in the shades used to protect royalty from the sun. It also has the essence of spirituality, as in a Jewish wedding or a Buddhist religious ceremony.

CANYON (ARROYO, DEFILE, GORGE, RAVINE, WASH)

Any canyon or ravine symbolizes both the depth of the unconscious mind and the discovery of what is hidden there. In a deep canyon you can see the layers of rock, which suggest the layers of material within your mind. You can thus see the layers in your mind—they are above ground, so to speak. Still, there is the suggestion of more to be discovered. Other dream elements associated with the canyon may relate to unconscious material that is currently emerging, or they may be suggesting relationships you previously did not recognize. The arroyo or wash suggests the dryness of the objective world that is occasionally flooded with feelings from the unconscious, while a river bed or canyon with a steady flow of water suggests a constant awareness of the relationship between conscious and unconscious activities. The amount of water suggests the amount of disturbance caused in the unconscious.

CAPRICORN

The zodiacal sign of the goat, Capricorn is the sign of the winter solstice. It indicates the ambitious practical energy needed to move out of the darkness of winter toward spring.

CAR (see FORD)

CARDINAL

A fat little red bird, the cardinal is a cheery sight on a wintery day. The word *cardinal* means first, so the bird can symbolize your placing yourself first in line, or considering yourself first for a change. This bird may also symbolize vitality, as it can survive the winter cold.

CASTLE

Because the castle is a walled community, it includes the nature of a house with the nature of an enclosed city. It is an elevated sort of house, indicating spiritual power. If it has a moat, the only entrances are above the water (through intelligence), on the water (via the emotions), or under the water (by instinct). What looks impregnable, then, becomes accessible via at least three avenues. In a dream it suggests that spiritual strength is accessible to you at this time. Other attributes of the castle expand on this theme.

CAT (COUGAR, LEOPARD) (*see also* JAGUAR, LION, MOUNTAIN LION)

The Egyptians associated the cat with the goddesses Isis and Bast and it is also a familiar of witches. Unlike the dog, the domestic cat's loyalty goes only about as far as the next meal or warm lap. They are good companions in spite of this because they do not demand attention. They remain mysterious and symbolize the night and the depths of a dream, and therefore the mystery you are facing in your waking life.

CATASTROPHE (DESTRUCTION, DISASTER) (*see also* CRISIS)

When a catastrophe happens in a dream, foretelling is only one of the possible meanings. Far more frequently is it true that the subconscious, not being governed by the same logical parameters as the conscious mind, has exaggerated a dream element for effect. Sometimes the dream is trying to tell you something and has to amplify the image until you pay attention. When you consider the catastrophe in your dream, scale down a flood to a trickle to measure the material world effect. In the same way scale down the feeling—rage to irritation, for example.

CAULDRON (*see* CUP, GOBLET)

CAVE (CAVERN, SUBTERRANEAN PLACES)

A cave or cavern, being underground, suggests a site or event occurring in the unconscious territory of your mind. A descent of any kind indicates travelling into unconscious territory, with the suggestion that something of value can be found there (as in buried treasure). Dream figures in a cave symbolize relatively less conscious elements of your personality that are coming together in some way.

CEILING(S)

To see a ceiling you must look up, which symbolizes a mental or spiritual perspective. The design and color of the ceiling indicates the clarity of your vision. A dark ceiling may mean that you have not been addressing the spiritual side of things recently. If the ceiling is well lit, you can see the details of your mental or spiritual work easily.

CELLAR (*see* BASEMENT)

CELTIC KNOT (*see* LABYRINTH)

CENTAUR

A mythical beast, part horse and part man, the centaur brings you face-to-face with your animal nature. In a dream the centaur reflects the power of your instinctual nature, and also indicates the unconscious realm. Understanding its message can set the stage for later spiritual development.

CENTER (*see* **CIRCLE, DISK**)

CERBERUS

This guardian of the underworld may also be a guardian of your own unconscious, signaling the barrier (or at least division) between conscious and less conscious activity. While this symbol may appear intimidating, you may actually be able to pass this barrier without serious difficulty. Cerberus serves to keep certain unconscious material from emerging, but will allow you to make that decision because you are at the gate itself in the dream. This would be an indication that you are at or near lucid dreaming.

CEREMONY (*see* **RITE**)

CHAIN (PLAIT) (*see also* **BRAIDS, CADUCEUS**)

Intertwined links suggest the caduceus. A chain also suggests the binding qualities of rope.

CHALICE (*see* **CUP, GOBLET**)

CHAMELEON

This animal changes its color to blend into its surroundings. In a dream a chameleon may be an indication that you should do the same, although you should not give up your integrity to do so.

CHAOS

Sometimes called the Void, chaos is the state of things before the creation of order occurs. It is associated with the unconscious, as both are dark and without differentiation. Any chaotic state in a dream symbolizes unconscious contents about to emerge into conscious awareness.

CHARIOT

Control is the key feature of any chariot depiction. The driver, a sentient being, must control, either directly or indirectly, the horses or other animals that pull the chariot. In a dream this image indicates that control is an important factor in your waking life.

CHECKERS

A checkerboard has spaces defined by squares of different colors and checker pieces move from one square to another. The pattern also includes diamond shapes and is symbolic of the duality or multiplicity of elements. Modern quilts contain a multiplicity of colors and designs. In a dream this kind of pattern symbolizes the variety of ideas and feelings that go into any personality.

CHERUBIM (*see* **ANGELS**)

CHICKADEE

A tiny bird, the chickadee's cheery call is like a sentinel, calling you to become aware of something unique and interesting in your life.

CHILD

Children are symbolic of purity, life, and the future. A child in a dream may also represent your inner child, a younger, possibly more simple version of your self.

CHIMERA

The chimera is a monster with a lion's head, a goat's body, and the tail of a dragon. Sometimes it breathes fire. Thought to be symbolic of evil, a chimera in a dream suggests confusion of forces and the need to sort out your thoughts and feelings.

CHOICE (*see also* CROSS, CROSSROADS, CRUCIFIXION)

When a choice is offered in a dream, it is an opportunity for you to take charge in the dream and begin lucid dreaming. It also symbolizes decisions to be made in your waking life. Examine the nature of the choice (not the content) to get a sense of how you may feel about the conscious choice you face and then offer a resolution.

CHRISTMAS (*see* YULE)

CHRYSALIS (COCOON)

The chrysalis and cocoon symbolize the protected state in which a transformative life experience occurs. In your dream they suggest the moment or period in which you undergo significant transformation. The look and feel of the chrysalis or cocoon indicate the nature of the transformation itself.

CIRCLE (CENTER, GRAPHICS) (*see also* DISK)

The circle and its center is possibly the most basic symbol of wholeness. All mandalic (round) figures participate in the symbolism of wholeness. At the same time the round object has its own meaning. Coins have specific monetary value, wheels make vehicles or machines move, and spheres can be planets or moons, crystal balls, or marbles. Art around the world incorporates mandalic representations of wholeness. Haloes suggest the spiritual completeness in religious art. Buddhist *thangkas* use the circle to define the limits of personal awareness and also to establish the measurements of the Buddha or guru figure. The circle defines a geometric center, and the mandala defines a personal, spiritual center.

CIRCLE WITH CROSS

A cross within a circle is the astrological symbol for the earth. It links the center with the circumference in the four primary directions, and thus can be viewed as a beacon of sorts, guiding you to your own center within the universe described by the circle. It is therefore symbolic of orientation or self-orientation.

City

A particular city in a dream calls your attention to experiences there, or to feelings you associate with that specific place. A more general association is with the workings of social and cultural life. Even if you have strong associations with the real city in question, don't forget to consider the feeling evoked in the dream.

Climate (Weather)

Climate and weather are metaphors for emotions. The mundane weather in your dream may be symbolic of your inner psychic weather. How do you feel about the element in the dream itself? How did you feel when you awoke, or when you were recording the dream? How does that feeling relate to your waking life?

Cloak

This article of clothing veils the dream character from you. The fabric and ornamentation symbolize the way you are prevented from seeing the dream figure's full reality. The cloak symbolizes a curtain or drape.

Clock

Time is an important aspect of waking life. We schedule all aspects of school, work, and play around the passage of time. The traditional clock in a dream is a kind of mandala, reminding you of the division of life into twelve facets. The modern digital clock allows for more numerous divisions, and also focuses on the mathematical accounting associated with time.

Clothes (Blouse, Tunic) (*see also* Shirt)

Regardless of the quality or type of clothing in dreams, it is the feeling it evokes that is significant. How do you feel when you consider the clothing of a particular dream figure?

Clouds

Clouds symbolize messages coming from beyond. They could be from prophets, spirit guides, or angels. They represent the realm of the mind. In terms of your dream weather, clouds can be interpreted as emotional indicators.

Clover

The three leaves of clover can symbolize past-present-future trinity or other trinities of similar ideas. The four-leafed clover is lucky because it shows you have taken the three parts of the creative *process* and arrived at the created *result*.

CLOWN

The clown represents the not-so-logical side of life. In a dream a clown symbolizes the Trickster who gets you to think about your problems and feelings in a different way—to see life differently.

CLUSTER (*see* BUNCH)

COAL

This concentrated source of energy is also the precursor of the brilliant diamond. In a dream coal symbolizes the raw state of things. Because it can become a diamond, it also symbolizes the pure potential of an alchemical process.

COBRA

The cobra is strongly associated with the power of creation. Its hypnotic power can alter your state of consciousness and help your creative forces emerge. The cobra pose in yoga serves to aid development of spine flexibility and the flow of kundalini energy.

COBWEB

A cobweb symbolizes a veil that conceals the truth.

COCK (ROOSTER)

The cock is a symbol of the sun and also of dawn. The cock symbol is often used on weather vanes. All those meanings share the qualities of vigilance and activity. The cock in a dream may signal a new upwelling of spirit within you, and a new dawn for your life. Expect positive changes.

COCOON (*see* CHRYSALIS)

COLD

Often when you are cold in a dream it is because the room in which you are sleeping is cold. Consider this possibility first when evaluating coldness in a dream. Then consider that cold is associated with the feeling of isolation. We sometimes use the word to describe a noncommunicative individual, so the feeling of coldness could reflect a sense you have about a person in the dream or in your waking life.

COLORS

The symbolism of color contains a vast richness of variety. It is important to associate the color with the dream object first. Thus a Chinese red jacket is possibly first red and second Chinese.

COLUMN

An isolated column symbolizes the mind's upward movement to achieve greater objectivity. Two columns may suggest a dichotomy in the material world and that choices must be made. A building composed of many columns has two inherent opposing values which alternate in an orderly fashion. In tarot and other contexts, the pillars represent mercy and severity and not as separate principals, but as two sides of a natural reality.

COMB (SIEVE)

A comb or sieve in a dream symbolizes of the sift-like process of evaluation and decision-making. It provides a metaphor for straightening or sorting out ideas and feelings.

COMPASS (see also DIRECTIONS)

A dream compass can indicate the metaphorical direction you should take on some matter of importance. It also encompasses all the directions of creation.

CONCORD (see AGREEMENT)

CONE

The cone is the basic shape of many things from a dunce cap to a witch's hat. You can shape a cone from a flat piece of paper by twisting it, so the cone incorporates an inherent three-dimensionality of a two-dimensional form. In a dream it may symbolize a transition from two-dimensional thinking to a level where synthesis of ideas and feelings occur. In many cases, the shape implies an upward or downward movement. This shape is also used to amplify the sound of the voice, or concentrate sounds so they can be heard more readily.

CONSTELLATION

A constellation is stars grouped together in patterns to form animals, objects, and mythological figures. When something else comes together in a constellation in a dream, or when you see a heavenly constellation, it indicates the mental process of gathering and amalgamating ideas and feelings into a complex working unit. Do the elements of your dream constellation make sense together? Sometimes unconscious constellations of ideas are difficult to understand or accept in consciousness because they include contradictory elements that you cannot resolve logically. The dream provides you with the logic of your unconscious, and thus offers a solution to the problem.

CONTAINER (see BOX)

CONTRAST (see INVERSION)

COPPER

This metal is associated with the planet Venus. It is known to have healing properties, and thus is worked into jewelry worn to relieve the pain of arthritis or other ailments. It conducts electricity easily so in a dream it may reflect your capacity to allow information to flow through your being.

CORAL

Coral is often associated with blood, and can be seen as a symbol of purification of the blood.

CORD (see ROPE)

CORN (see MAIZE)

CORNUCOPIA

This form symbolizes the union of the masculine and feminine. The outside of the form is phallic, while the inside is hollow and represents the female form. The union of these forms symbolizes the abundance of all creation. The dream symbol points to the fact that you have prosperity in your life in areas associated with other dream content.

COUGAR (see CAT, JAGUAR, LION, MOUNTAIN LION)

COW (see BULL, OX)

COYOTE

The coyote in a dream indicates that the Trickster archetype is at work. American Indian stories about the coyote all indicate that he is intelligent and able to manipulate situations. The Trickster appears to us when we need to see things differently—when we have limited our perspective to just one side of a situation. There is magic in trickster energy. You may be at a juncture where you can make big changes easily, if you just redirect your attention and see more than one side of a problem. The Trickster reminds us that we have psychic depths that we have yet to fully understand.

CRANE

Cranes are prominent in art objects around the world. Generally long-lived, they also mate for life. Martial arts include the crane form which combines the art of balance and the ability to strike with deadly accuracy. The crane may be indicating that you should focus your energies on one endeavor rather than dividing your forces.

CREATION

A dream about the creation of the world or the creation of any material thing symbolizes the creative energy of mind being translated into material works. The dream image shows you that the moment is at hand to manifest something of your ideas and desires.

CREMATION (BURNING)

In alchemy burning something is symbolic of purifying the essential substance. Thus a dream image of a person being cremated suggests the ultimate release from the imperfect body into the perfection of spirit. Are you undergoing a "trial by fire"? Perhaps you are becoming aware of a part of yourself that is being purified by a difficult test.

CRESCENT

The crescent form is reminiscent of the moon and her phases and represents the changeable character of things. It also represents the feminine principle at work in your dream.

CRICKET (GRASSHOPPER)

The cricket may be a trickster image, as the cricket's sound can seem to be coming from first one place, then another. The Chinese believed the cricket was a sign of good cheer. The cricket or grasshopper is a symbol of movement, and indicates in the dream that movement is occurring, or about to occur. It signals you to prepare to move forward happily. It also tells you to listen to your inner voice.

CRISIS (DESTRUCTION, DISASTER) (see also CATASTROPHE)

Any crisis event in a dream indicates that in your waking life you are reaching the crisis point in some arena. Recalling that the unconscious tends to exaggerate things, a huge dream crisis may be associated with a relatively minor conscious one. The essence is in the twist or turning of the action—some action on your part is necessary to move the situation forward. Dream disasters and catastrophes indicate a crisis point, but usually do not forebode such a dire outcome in your waking life. Rather, the nature of the dream event suggests the emotional value or importance of your decision.

CROCODILE (see ALLIGATOR)

CRONOS

This god symbolizes the passage of time. It may also indicate realms beyond time. Because dreams often represent a different time continuum, Cronos points to the relative passage of time as a key factor in your dream, and thus in your life.

CROSS (see also CHOICE, CROSSROADS, CRUCIFIXION)

The cross is a symbol that spans cultures and ethnic groups all over the world. It represents the four directions. It is the mathematical symbol for addition, and thus symbolizes all conditions in which the additive property dwells. It is the principal symbol of Christianity. It also lies at the center of the swastika, a symbol important to Hinduism as well as to the Nazi Party.

CROSSROADS (*see also* CHOICE, CROSS, CRUCIFIXION)

The crossroads is a definitive symbol of a choice you are attempting to make on both the conscious and unconscious levels. It also is symbolic of the union of forces calling for the decision. Try to identify the active, neutral, and passive energies at play in your decision-making process.

CROW

The crow indicates that natural laws are significant at this time. The crow brings the message of the law to you. Yet crows are notorious shape-shifters, and you may experience them first one way and then another. The crow is therefore symbolic of magical or spiritual strength.

CROWD

A crowd in a dream symbolizes active movement in the unconscious realm. Do you feel like there is a lot going on inside? Perhaps you feel like there are many personalities active inside, and not the unified being you tend to feel like consciously.

CROWN (*see also* HEADDRESS)

The crown symbolizes preeminence or success. In a dream any figure with a crown can symbolize some part of yourself.

CRUCIFIXION (*see also* CHOICE, CROSS, CROSSROADS)

The crucifixion of Christ served to bridge the gap between humanity and divinity. In a dream a crucifixion symbolizes the ambivalence we feel when we cannot make a decision. The horizontal and vertical parts of the cross symbolize the paradoxical factors you are facing. Can you define the opposite arguments clearly? Then imagine them together as part of the cross and try to see how they may be joined in synthesis.

CRUTCH

In a dream a crutch may symbolize a dream figure's need for support, or it may symbolize an area of your life where you need support.

CRYSTAL

Any crystal participates in the solidity of form and the transparency of mind. Various crystalline substances are thought to have certain properties: the diamond is valued for its hardness and its clarity, for example. The color and type of crystal may evoke a certain feeling in the dream, which indicates its nature.

CUBE

This geometric shape forms the basis for most construction, as it is the basic unit of all building materials. It is solid, grounded, and stable, and represents those qualities in a dream. It indicates a consolidation of the elements of fire, earth, air, and water into one form.

CUCKOO

The cuckoo is a symbol of timing or fate—an indication of a change in direction.

CUP (CAULDRON, CHALICE) (*see also* GOBLET)

The cauldron and chalice are both containers of transformational forces. The chalice is associated with Christian churches, while the cauldron is a Celtic symbol. The vessels themselves contain the base material to be used, while the space above them represents the spiritual forces to be invoked. The cauldron focuses on material "work," while the chalice suggests mental or spiritual work. Any similar container suggests the containment of matter and the spaciousness of spirit. These containers are symbolic of destiny. The nature of the container itself suggests meaning, and its contents are of great importance.

CURL (LOOP) (*see also* BODY, HAIR, HEAD, KNOT)

A curl of hair or a loop of string or rope indicates binding, like a knot, even though there is no actual knot.

CURTSY (*see* BOW)

CURTAIN (DRAPE)

Just as window curtains in waking life separate a room from the outside world, so do they symbolize separation in a dream. Any action in the dream to open or remove the curtain is an act of penetrating a mystery. What is behind the curtain in the dream? The curtain is a most significant element, as it indicates what you need to understand more fully.

CYBELE

Cybele is a wife of Saturn who personified earth energy. The seven-pointed star is associated with this goddess as a symbol of the cyclic progression of life. The crescent moon is also associated with her as a symbol for the appearance and disappearance of material forms in the night or subconscious worlds.

CYCLE

A cycle represents a series of events or the time frame in which the series occurs. In a dream any cyclical action may be a reminder of the cyclical patterns of all life. The cyclic pattern suggests a beginning and an end which returns you to the beginning, or at least to a new beginning point.

CYCLONE (*see* BREEZE, HURRICANE, WIND)

CYCLOPS

Cyclops is a one-eyed giant in Greek mythology. In a dream it may indicate the single-minded focus of the dream figure, as well as the risk of becoming overly focused on one goal.

CYPRESS

The cypress tree is often associated with death and the underworld. In a dream this may be associated with a trip into the underworld of the unconscious mind. The term *cypress* is also used for the black gauze drapes of mourning.

DANCE

Dancing symbolizes the act of creation and transformation. Dancing joins energies together in a magical way. Some dances symbolize of the transformation from a human being into a god. Rhythmic dance moves you into an altered state of mind. In a dream the dance suggests change or a transitional time period in your waking life.

DARKNESS

Some dreams that seem to occur at night or in darkness are actually in black and white. You may want to consider this possibility, especially if you normally dream in color. Once you have established that the dream element is true darkness, think about what area of your life is in its beginning stages, before your efforts have produced any concrete results. How does the feeling of the dream relate to that area of your life? The dream may be trying to reveal some information or skill that could be helpful.

DEATH

While it is possible that a dream image of death can foretell something, this is relatively rare. Usually death in your dreams relates to the ending of one activity and the beginning of something new. It can be seen as a positive symbol because you need to create space for new activities, and thus need to complete old ones. Death dreams often stimulate powerful emotional reactions, and this represents the energy you have to put into a new project. How strong is the feeling in the dream? How can you apply the energy of that emotion to your waking life?

DECAPITATION

Decapitation symbolizes the feeling of being separated from your spiritual self. Since such a separation is really not possible, you may want to consider how you can regain the feeling of spiritual alignment, or how you can help others to regain theirs.

DECORATIONS

Decorations for parties and holidays symbolize celebration. Medals symbolize spiritual elevation or the attainment of objectivity after some struggle.

DEER (FAWN)

The deer is shy and gentle and uses its loving disposition to capture your heart. Its message may be to exercise love and compassion in your waking life. The deer appears in Buddhist art as a companion of the Buddha. The deer is alert on both the physical and the psychic level and is sensitive to the energies around it. The fawn, like any infant, indicates the newly born or discovered quality of the adult animal.

DEFILE (see CANYON)

DELUGE (see also OCEAN, RAIN, RAINBOW, REEFS, RIVER, WATER, WAVE, WETNESS)

A downpour of rain in a dream symbolizes both the destructive qualities of storms and the purifying quality of water. On the destructive side you may feel overwhelmed by dream images. On the purifying side you may find that upon examination, these images supply missing information that helps you resolve a question in your waking life.

DESERT (DRYNESS)

The arid desert symbolizes the more objective view of the intellect, as opposed to the watery condition of the unconscious mind. The sun rules there, and the sun symbolizes spiritual radiance. Thus the desert in your dream may indicate your search for or your discovery of the spirit within yourself. The desert feels like a dry wasteland sometimes, and you may find that you need to inject life into your spiritual quest in some way. Desert dryness implies the existence of fire—the element that symbolizes intuition. Think of intuition as bare—not robed in any decoration. Is there a feature of the desert or dry place in the dream that informs your intuition?

DESTRUCTION (see CATASTROPHE, CRISIS)

DEVIL

The Devil in tarot represents a moment when you feel unable to make a decision. You feel bound, although the figures in this card are so loosely bound that they could easily escape. You may feel that you are stagnating in your waking life in some way because of a lack of decision. The card also symbolizes desire and its control over your intellect.

DIAMOND

The diamond comes from the same source as coal, but is the hardest and purest form of carbon. It has come to represent pure love between partners. It also symbolizes the pure being that emerges from the developmental processes of psychological or alchemical work. In baseball the diamond is the shape of the infield. This field may symbolize the purity of the stone in a dream. The diamond is an equilateral four-sided figure that typically contains angles not equal to ninety degrees. This shape is used in road signs to indicate upcoming hazards. The diamond's shape is typically oriented to the cardinal directions. It may symbolize the direction toward purification. The diamond shape is an integral part of the religious art of the Maya, who used it to define the proportion of all things physical and spiritual. Diamonds symbolize perfection. In Hindu and Buddhist writings, the diamond symbolizes the light of realization in all its perfection. In a dream the diamond symbolizes that which is lasting and perfected. How does it relate to you in your waking life?

DIANA (see also HECATE)

The goddess Diana is a huntress and is related to the moon, and therefore to the night. In a dream she may symbolize the part of you seeking an answer to some question, or the solution to a problem. Diana can become Hecate, the Terrible Mother, or all that is frightening about the female. These two symbols together are expressions of the pure, directed feminine force which is contrasted with our tumultuous emotions in waking life. Each goddess implies the existence of the others. How can you harness your emotions so they work for you instead of against you?

DIGESTION (EATING) (see also FOOD)

Eating and digestion in dreams represents the movement within the mind from raw materials (facts, feeling, and intuition) to wisdom. Food in dreams represents an offering from your unconscious. It is auspicious to eat what is offered, even if you are afraid in the dream, as you can then "digest" the meaning of the offering. Look beyond the actual food to what it symbolizes for you personally.

DIONYSUS (see also PAN)

The gods Dionysus or Pan in a dream may be the embodiment of an unconscious desire that is emerging into consciousness. Take a moment to reflect on the dream image. Does it speak to you? Does it reveal what the desire is? The sexual associations with these figures may be pertinent, but perhaps not. Examine this symbol in terms of desire, without focusing on the sexual connotation, and you may find the significance.

DIRECTIONS (*see also* COMPASS)

Compass directions serve to orient the traveler. In a dream they indicate the life direction you are taking. The compass generally takes the form of a mandala and therefore suggests wholeness.

DISAPPEARANCE

When something disappears or is missing in a dream, it may be because it has a quality you are not willing to look at. Think about the missing person or object. What is it about it you find distasteful? An honest assessment will only reveal your humanness, as we all find less likable qualities in the people and things we value most. If you are willing to consider what you dislike about the missing thing, you put yourself on the path to wholeness.

DISASTER (*see* CATASTROPHE, CRISIS)

DISGUISE (MASK)

A disguise or mask symbolizes the paradoxical nature of something. If you disguise yourself, you wish to appear different from the way you are. The disguise or mask represents the quality being sought. Examine it in detail to discover more about that quality. What can you do in your waking life to achieve the change you seek in the dream? The mask also symbolizes secrecy. Are you doing something that calls for secrecy?

DISK (CENTER, GRAPHICS) (*see also* CIRCLE)

Any disk or circle symbolizes the sun, the energy of life, and perfect wholeness.

DISMEMBERMENT

A dream image that is dismembered or incomplete can be a simple symbol for procreation, as the infant is separated from the body of the mother. It can also represent the feeling of loss of something that was as important as a part of your own body. Third, it can stand for the movement from unity to multiplicity. In spite of the painful or dire image of dismemberment, it is potentially a very positive sign that you are moving in a productive direction in your waking life.

DISTORTION (*see* MALFORMATION)

DOG

A dog in a dream indicates loyalty in your life. Dogs have been domesticated since earliest recorded history and provide companionship without questioning our judgment. If the dog is prominent in your dream or waking life, examine your loyalty to others and theirs to you. Recognizing your loyalty to a principal can be important also. Unlike the coyote, the dog in a dream is not a trickster symbol. Nor do they have the wolf's powerful psychic energy.

DOLL (DUMMY, PUPPET)

Dolls and puppets are extensions of ourselves. We dress them, play with them, and allow them to act out scenarios for us. In dreams they symbolize something that we might like to act out, but have not done in waking life. Are you projecting some feeling or desire onto the doll or puppet in your dream? What is the doll doing and how does it parallel your desires? Do you feel like a puppet in the dream or in your waking life, being manipulated by someone else? How can you become the puppet master yourself? The doll has a magical quality—it can become a playmate or it can even become a container for thoughts and feelings that we choose not to carry around consciously.

DOLPHIN (*see also* PORPOISE)

The dolphin inhabits deep water and thus symbolizes the dream world or unconscious mind. Yet the dolphin breathes the same air we do. It can indicate that you can have fun exploring the unconscious world of dreams to learn about another side of your being. It also emphasizes the rhythm of the breath in its swimming, and reminds us to breathe freely and rhythmically.

DOMINIONS (*see* ANGELS)

DONKEY (*see* ASS)

DOOR

The archetypal door is a feminine symbol, as it is the entrance to a space, as compared to a wall, which delimits the space. Doors represent access to all within, and therefore are symbolic of intelligence. They also are symbolic of change and transition from one place or state to another. Finally, they are the archetypal entrance to the self or soul, symbolized by the building itself.

DOUBLE (DUALISM) (*see also* TWINS)

Any doubling symbolizes the duality inherent in the material world. The paired things can be identical, or they can be obvious opposites, or they can have the tricky quality of appearing identical while acting in opposite ways. A double of yourself may symbolize your spiritual or unconscious being—a component of yourself that is always there to support you through whatever experiences you encounter. How do you feel about the double in your dream? That is a key to apply to your waking life.

DOUBLE SPIRAL

DNA is a double spiral, moving both clockwise and counterclockwise. It symbolizes the interaction of opposite forces in the act of creation. The movement between the opposites is just as significant as the forward movement they maintain.

DOVE

A sign of peace and the love of God, the dove also symbolizes the Holy Spirit. The dove returned to Noah with an olive branch, signaling the end of the Deluge. The song of the dove evokes sadness. This symbol presents a paradox of mourning and new life, and may signal a paradoxical shift in your waking life.

DRAGON

The mythical dragon breathes fire and flies on filmy wings. It has reptilian features and harks back to ancient times. (In fact, the back of the brain is called the reptilian brain—ancient indeed!) Dragons in legend are the enemy, to be fought and slain. On the other hand, in modern lore the dragon is symbolic of the power of the elements. The Chinese dragon symbolized the power of the emperor, and it became one of the twelve Chinese zodiacal signs. A dragon in your dreams speaks to an inherent primitive life force available to you. While some psychologists regard the dragon as evil, you will find that yours can become a friendly source of energy.

DRAGONFLY

American Indian lore links this river creature to the dragon, with its unusual color and general appearance. It is, like other insects, symbolic of change, as it undergoes metamorphosis from a water animal to a denizen of the air. The dragonfly symbolizes change when it appears in your dream or waking life. It may be suggesting you need to deal with an illusion that has taken over part of your life.

DRAPE (*see* CURTAIN)

DRUM

The drum symbolizes the heart—the physical heart or the metaphorical heart of something. It incorporates symbols of life (the tree and skins from which it is made), the feminine aspect (the dark interior), and the power of communication. What do the shape and appearance of the drum suggest about the nature of the dream? What do they communicate to you?

DRYNESS (*see* DESERT)

DUALISM (*see* DOUBLE, TWINS)

DUCK (GANDER, GOOSE)

Ducks are friendlier than geese. Both are feminine symbols, and both indicate the potential to dip beneath the surface of the unconscious to nurture yourself. Graceful in both water and air, these birds are less oriented to the practical limitations of the earth element. The relationship between air and water is the relationship between intellect and feeling, thought and judgment.

DUMBNESS

The inability to speak in a dream suggests regression to an earlier time, when you were too young to speak, or too uninformed to have anything to say. It can be frightening—you feel a need to call out but no sound comes out. Examine how the inability to communicate feels in the dream. How do you generally protect yourself from this feeling? How can you help a future dream figure to speak?

DUMMY (*see* DOLL)

DWARF

A dwarf symbolizes the gateway to the unconscious. What he or she says and does in the dream is indicative of the nature and condition of the path from waking to dreaming. The dwarf is both guardian and guide.

E

EAGLE (BALD EAGLE)

The eagle is connected to the Great Spirit or the divine. The feathers are valued as spiritual tools. The Aztec god Quetzalcoatl is also known as the "feathered serpent" and is depicted as an eagle with a serpent in its beak. The spirit of the eagle in your dream addresses courage and power. The eagle soars high above the earth and has highly developed vision. In your dream it may be symbolic of your spiritual vision, which may be truer than your ordinary eyesight. In many parts of the world the eagle is associated with the gods, nobility, and powerful positions. Although the eagle is generally associated with the air element, it is also a symbol for the sign of Scorpio.

EAR

Both the human ear and the ear of corn symbolize the capacity to hear. The ear of corn is symbolic of fertility. Its many kernels suggest the ability to hear in different ways. In a dream either symbol can suggest the desirability of listening without judging, as well as hearing what is underneath the obvious meaning.

EARTH

While the sun is the source of the energy needed for life, it is the earth that provides the container for life. The condition of the earth in your dream suggests the opinion of your unconscious mind about the condition of your relationship to life. A desolate image may mean you are feeling alone or unproductive. A rich image suggests the opposite. Your feeling in the dream when you look at the image is significant, and you may want to consider changes in your waking life to improve negative feelings.

EARTHQUAKE

We think of the earth as being stable and constant, but the earthquake proves that is not always the case. In a dream the earthquake symbolizes a massive shift in the unconscious. Remember, though, that a huge dream image is analogous to a much smaller shift in the waking world. Is there anything you find in the dream that is demanding your attention by being associated with the earthquake?

EAST

East is the direction of the past. If you travel east in a dream, you are often able to revisit the past and gather information.

EATING (*see* DIGESTION, FOOD)

EDEN (*see* FALL)

EFFIGY

An effigy is a likeness of the real thing. In a dream an effigy symbolizes the feeling of only being a stand-in, and not being real in your own right. Another possible meaning is that you create the dream effigy because you cannot subject the real person to the feelings you have for him or her. For example, if you burn the dream figure in a rage, you do so in lieu of actually harming that person. Such a dream image serves to reduce the real person's power over you, or to satisfy your yearning for the person. In both situations the dream is allowing you to experience the compensating feeling and to gain understanding of ambivalent feelings. Does the effigy represent a specific person, but stand for something else—perhaps a feeling?

EGG

The egg symbolizes fertility and life. It suggests the potential of something, as well as immortality as a concept. The egg is a container for both matter and for thought. What does your dream egg contain?

EGYPT

Egypt symbolizes the roots of feeling and civilization. As such it has a primitive quality. In a dream it represents a return to a time when life was simpler *and* when you may have felt closer to your spiritual side.

EIGHT

The figure eight is a lemniscate—a figure that eternally revolves into itself. It includes two circles or ellipses but is one object. The Tibetan Wheel of Law, or *Dharma Chakra,* the lotus, the eightfold Buddhist path, and numerous other sets of sacred symbols contain eight elements. The Chinese believe eight is the number of prosperity. When the eight appears in a dream you may consider your intuition as a strong source of valuable information.

ELEMENTS

The alchemical elements (fire, earth, air, water, and ether) symbolize the psychological building blocks of personality (intuition, sensation, feeling, and thinking). Fire is the element of the Holy Spirit in Christianity and of spirits in other religions. Spirit often comes to use in the form of intuition. Water is the element associated with the unconscious, where thoughts and feelings flow freely, unhampered by psychological constructs (complexes). Air is associated with intellect and logic. Earth is associated with sensation and the material world.

ELEPHANT

Elephants are long-lived and because of this symbolize wisdom. They are strong and powerful—strong enough, some cultures say, to support the world itself. The story of Dumbo is a continuation of the myth that elephants can fly from other cultures. Ganesa is a Hindu deity with an elephant's head, and is imbued with the qualities of education and wisdom. He is a man who obtained the elephant head by defending his mother Parvati, being slain, and being resuscitated as a reward for his loyalty.

ELEVATOR (*see* STAIRS, STEPS)

ELK

Strength and endurance are the elk's powers. The elk is a social animal (note the men's organization by the same name). For both sexes, elk in a dream may indicate you are or should be associating with people of the same gender. If you are under a lot of stress, eat elk food—vegetables mostly, to lighten the feeling of being weighed down.

EMBLEMS

An emblem is a symbol designed to represent something else. In a dream a familiar emblem may loosely symbolize something else also associated with the thing it normally represents. The value of the emblem may increase in value through its association with a symbol as well.

EMPEROR

The Emperor of tarot symbolizes the completion of creative work. He holds the tools that have been used, and sits upon a cube-shaped throne which symbolizes the work itself. The details of this figure and his surroundings suggest the nature of the work created.

EMPRESS

The Empress of tarot symbolizes a creative work in progress. She has the capacity for the work and the necessary tools. She is imbued with living energy. The details of this figure and her surroundings suggest the nature of the creative work in progress.

EMPTINESS (VOID) (*see also* ABYSS, MACROCOSM, NOTHINGNESS, SPACE)

Emptiness is symbolic of the moment before creation. It is the space from which everything emerges into consciousness. A feeling of emptiness in a dream thus symbolizes the creative process at work.

ENCHANTMENT

Enchantment symbolizes a movement downward into the subconscious realms. While it can be seen as a form of punishment, it represents a gathering of force that occurs within the psyche.

ENCLOSURE (CAGE)

An enclosure or cage in a dream symbolizes the feeling of limitation and restriction associated with negative emotions such as grief, humiliation, and shame. It can be seen as a suitable place for such negative emotions, or as a way to keep them from emerging into consciousness. The key to the meaning is what's in the cage. How do you relate to the caged persona or animal? What can it tell you about yourself?

ENIGMA (PARADOX) (*see also* INVERSION)

An enigma or paradox symbolizes the mysterious, dual nature of everything in the material world. If you can look at the two sides and see how they are related or part of one unity, then you resolve the paradox and can use the energy of that pair effectively.

ENTANGLEMENT (SNARE, WEB)
(*see also* NET, SPIDER, SPIDER WOMAN, SPINNING, WEAVING)

The entanglement symbolizes the return to or connection with the maternal quality (as with the umbilical cord). In a dream, then, any entanglement suggests the need to return to the feminine principle to find the answer to the puzzle. It suggests the limitation of logic and intellect, and the importance of feeling and intuition.

EROTICISM (SEXUAL IMAGES)

Freud suggested that many dream images relate to sexuality. Oranges may represent the breast, while cucumbers have an obvious phallic shape. The orange may also simply be an orange, or it may arouse an erotic sensation, or both. Because dreams are so personal, it is very important to assess how you feel about your erotic dream images. Consider how you felt during the dream, and also how you felt when you awoke, and while you were recording the dream. The changes in feeling as you go through these steps are often significant. For example, you might feel sexually aroused in the dream, ashamed upon awaking, but relieved after you record and think about the dream, and it may not be possible to understand why your feelings changed.

ESCALATOR (see STAIRS, STEPS)

ESPALIER (BONSAI TREE)

Decorative trees can be trimmed into special shapes, or they can be trained to grow next to a wall. In both cases their shape depends on the conscious shaping by human effort. The decorative tree, left to its own devices, can outgrow its shape. The life of an espalier tree depends on the wall, and the tree would fall and break without it. This tree has a two-dimensional existence that mirrors a black-and-white approach to the material world. The decorative tree in your dream suggests some limitation based on conscious thought, without due consideration to instinct or nature.

ETERNITY

Any long period of time in a dream symbolizes a period of waiting, which can feel like a very long time when you are the one waiting. An eternally occurring or repetitive process symbolizes the process of rumination, which can sometimes lead to boredom with the subject, but which can also lead to deeper understanding.

EUPHRATES

The Euphrates River and the land near it is known as the birthplace of civilization. Thus it symbolizes fertility, and suggests the fertility of the subconscious mind.

EVE

Eve, the first woman, symbolizes physical form. As first woman, Eve represents the material, fertile aspect of life. In contrast to the Virgin Mary or other spiritual mothers, Eve symbolizes natural mothering roles.

EXCREMENT (POOP)

Excrement symbolizes the gross and impure, but by reflection represents the pure, or the process of purification. What is associated with excrement in the dream? That may be what you are trying to purify in the material world. It also symbolizes waste products that are no longer necessary. It could relate to leftover material in a manufacturing process, for example. However, just as mine tailings contain residual metals, excrement has value, not the least of which is to fertilize new growth. Do you have ideas or plans that can grow in the waste of a previous project?

Extraordinary Abilities (Flying, Telekinesis, Telepathy, Time Travel)

Extraordinary capabilities in dreams have several meanings: (1) They may represent wish fulfillment: flying in a dream may symbolize the wish to be free; (2) They may represent latent abilities or an ability which can be expressed on the astral plane. Travel back or forward in time is thought to be a reality on the astral plane, for example; (3) They may relate to the world in the dream event, and not so much to the ability involved. For example, telekinesis may be a dream vehicle for delivering information about moving objects; and (4) The dream ability may incorporate a message for you. The ability to sense what other people are thinking or feeling may symbolize the need to pay more attention to what people are telling you in words, body language, and action.

Eye

The eye symbolizes the soul. In a dream eyes may reflect your state of mind in the dream.

Fairies

Because fairies represent something supernatural or magical, they are symbolic of powers you possess or wish to possess that are presently outside your awareness.

Falcon (*see* Hawk, Sparrow Hawk)

Fall (Accident, Autumn, Eden)

Fall is the season of harvest and preparation for winter. It symbolizes wisdom that develops out of experience. Dream figures in autumn settings may be seen as teachers or guides. The fall of Adam and Eve from the Garden of Eden symbolizes the separation we feel from oneness, or God. The fall may symbolize any separation you are experiencing. Falling in a dream rarely foretells a serious accident. Rather, it symbolizes the fear of not succeeding in a task. Such a dream could be a literal depiction of falling in love. A gradual fall can indicate a descent into the realm of the unconscious, where you can gather valuable information.

FAN

The fan symbolizes circulation—of air, certainly, but also of feelings and thoughts. The speed of an electric fan suggests the rate of this circulation. A traditional hand-held fan symbolizes a weapon—either in a battle of love, when it reveals the holder's emotions, or in a physical battle, when it can be used to cut or jab an opponent. Because the principal element is air, the power lies in the intellect.

FARM/FARMER

Farms and farming symbolize a connection to and an understanding of the earth. It relates to practical activities and may indicate that you are in the midst of an ongoing activity that has yet to bear fruit.

FASTENER (*see* BOLT)

FATHER

The father in a dream can, of course, be himself. He may also represent the responsibility and authority in your life. There is an emphasis on the conscious side of your life. The father relates to time, law, and moral principles.

FAWN (*see* DEER)

FEAR

Dream images and situations are frequently frightening, either within the dream or upon awakening. They can be clues to events in the waking world that demand more careful attention and caution. They can also be dramatically amplified bits of reality that the dream projects in larger than life dimensions so that they will be noticed, rather like your best friend first tapping on your door, and then pounding louder when you fail to respond. Fear also means concern or reverence, so a fearful dream object may be one you find awesome, or that you need to protect in some way.

FEATHER

The feather symbolizes a quality of the personality. When it appears in a dream, it points to a quality exemplified by the characters or tone of the dream. It may also represent a gift that comes from the bird. Frequently the quality is authority or love.

FEMININITY

Feminine figures in dreams are who they are, but they may also symbolize archetypal feminine roles—Maiden, Mother, Temptress, Crone (Wise Old Woman). Does your dream figure stimulate ideas or feelings about the feminine side of your character? Your life?

FEN (*see* MARSH)

FERRET (*see* **WEASEL**)

FIELDS
Open fields symbolize the spaciousness of the mind and the breadth of potential available.

FIGHT
A physical fight or struggle symbolizes an emotional or mental struggle to make a decision. The details provide insight into the problem and your unconscious understanding of its complexity. Victory suggests a resolution, at least in the unconscious arena.

FIRE
Fire in a dream symbolizes contact with the intuitive side of your nature. What is the fire saying to you? What is the emotion associated with it?

FIRST MATTER (*see* **PRIME MATTER**)

FISH
A fish indicates the ability to live amid the contents of the unconscious mind. In a dream it may indicate that you are becoming more comfortable in the unconscious realm, or that there is information there that you need or desire. The fish also symbolizes Christianity, and two fish form the symbol for Pisces, the twelfth sign of the zodiac.

FISHING
Fishing symbolizes casting into the unconscious for wisdom. As such it represents a conscious effort to establish or to re-establish a connection with your own instinctual nature.

FIVE
The number five is associated with the pentagram. It is also the extension of four points into a center. The ancient Greeks found its proportions so satisfying that they used the number five to establish the golden mean. Five-pointed patterns are found throughout nature in the arrangement of seeds within fruits, the ratios involved in the growth of certain shelled animals, and the basic counting systems of antiquity. It symbolizes the principle of expansion.

FLAG (BANNER)
The color and images of the flag symbolize a message from your unconscious mind. It indicates that messages are emerging from the dream mind in a coded form, and they are considered important enough to be made into insignia.

FLAME
The flame symbolizes the spirit. In Christian theology the Holy Spirit appears in fire. The essence of the flame is intuition.

FLEUR-DE-LIS (*see also* BEE)

The bee, sometimes shown as the stylized heraldic fleur-de-lis, symbolizes industriousness. Either the flower or the insect indicates that your efforts are understood at the unconscious level, and that they are being encouraged. This symbol appears in coats of arms and in Egyptian royal decorations.

FLIGHT (FLYING) (*see also* EXTRAORDINARY ABILITIES)

Any dream action that takes you up into the air symbolizes the attainment of a more objective or far-seeing position. It also relates to the achievement of a somewhat superior position. Flying is sometimes a signal that you are entering a lucid dream—that you can control the progress of the dream. Did you feel in control when you were flying?

FLOCK (GROUP, HERD, MULTIPLICITY)

A group of dream elements symbolizes multiple interpretations or meanings. It suggests that the dream image, whatever it is, has many levels of significance to you. Some dream books suggest that this is a negative quality, as it indicates a lack of objectivity. However, for women, at least, the animus often appears as a group of men, and they are potentially very helpful psychically. Consider the organization and feel of the group as well as the nature of the symbol as you analyze this dream element.

FLOGGING (BEATING)

A beating symbolizes an unconscious need to purify yourself in some way. Do you know why the beating occurred in the dream? Even if you are not the object of the flogging, you may be able to see an area of your life that is out of balance. The reason for the dream beating may suggest a method of conscious adjustment.

FLOOR

When we are awake we think of the floor as a solid support that divides vertical space. In a dream, the floor and its nature may indicate something about how we experience the division between our waking life and the unconscious of dreams. A polished wood floor may indicate a well-kept barrier, or it may indicate an awareness of the separation between conscious and unconscious territory.

FLOWERS

Flowers are symbolic in their essence (or perfume) and their shape. Essentially circular flowers remind us of the mandala, the symbol of wholeness. Lily-shaped flowers suggest the feminine, birth, or rebirth. The color of the flower suggests additional meanings.

FLUTE

This ancient instrument was used by the gods to make music. It has a somewhat mournful sound, and may symbolize sadness. The modern flute is sprightly and light, and symbolizes rapid movement.

FLYING (*see* **EXTRAORDINARY ABILITIES, FLIGHT**)

FOG (*see* **MIST**)

FOOD (**EATING**) (*see also* **DIGESTION**)

Psychological lore suggests that it is best to eat food offered to you in a dream. The food symbolizes a source of nurturing or wisdom that your dream is offering. Food may symbolize the potential feast that is available if you consider your dream life as a significant factor in your waking life.

FOOL (**MINSTREL**)

The Fool of tarot may appear when you are starting out on a new journey. The nature of his (or her) clothing and the surroundings provide information about how the unconscious sees the new enterprise. The more consistent this traveler is with your conscious look and feel, the more balance there is between the parts of your personality. The more different the Fool's appearance, the greater need to analyze your path carefully.

FOOT

Feet allow us movement in the physical world. On the mental and emotional plane they provide understanding. On the spiritual plane they provide the foundation for all of our efforts. Pain or injury to the foot symbolizes stress on all levels of being.

FOOTPRINTS

Footprints symbolize an element of the divine acting in your dream.

FOOTWEAR

Shoes and other footwear symbolize the quality and degree of your understanding of dream elements. The bare foot suggests less understanding, or the beginning of a new path. Sturdy footwear suggests durability of the dream ideas. Slippers suggest comfort, dressy shoes suggest elegance, but also a somewhat limited purpose. Consider what you know of the uses of the type of footwear you find in the dream.

FORD (**CAR, STREAM**)

The Ford automobile suggests utility and accessibility. Any vehicle can represent your own physical body in a dream, and its quality may reflect something about your physical health and vitality. To ford a stream or river means to cross it or pass from one state of reality into another. The nature of the water (calm trickle or raging flood) indicates the emotional risk involved in this transition. Can you see anything in the water? Anything there may symbolize something that is emerging from the unconscious for your consideration in making the transition.

FOREST

A forest, especially deep within it, symbolizes the unconscious mind. What you see within the forest can be understood as a message or a gift from that part of yourself. As you accept such gifts, the forest ceases to be so dark and dangerous, and instead becomes a rich, fertile ground for emotional and spiritual growth.

FOSSIL

To a degree the fossil represents death, but more importantly it symbolizes that which lasts.

FOUNDATION

The foundation of a building is the base on which it is built. In a dream the foundation symbolizes your belief system, and its quality indicates how you relate to this part of your life unconsciously. A shifting foundation, for instance, indicates that you are in the process of changing your beliefs about something. A solid foundation of the proper size for the building indicates that you are well prepared, both consciously and unconsciously, for the tasks ahead of you.

FOUNTAIN

The fountain symbolizes the inner source of your being. It represents the flow of information from deep within your mind into consciousness. It also symbolizes the life-force of your ideas and feelings. Regardless of its appearance when you first see the dream symbol, if you work with it, the water will flow more clearly and the fountain itself will undergo change in a positive direction.

FOUR

Four symbolizes the apparent solidity of the material world. Because of the lasting nature of the physical objects we create, the number four is associated with achievements that exist outside the self and endure into the future. It is the traditional number of the elements, the Gospels, and the seasons. It is often associated with the square and the cube.

FOX

The fox is clever and resourceful. It can conceal itself to gain the advantage in hunting for food. It may indicate that you can benefit from concealing your thoughts, remaining silent, and observing the processes around you. The archetypal Trickster can appear as a fox, tricking you into seeing (or not seeing) something important about yourself.

FRACTURE (see also BROKEN OBJECTS)

Any dream object that is broken suggests an opening between the visible and invisible worlds. The object itself has its own symbolism, and the fracture suggests there are multiple significant meanings.

Frog

The frog is amphibious, and indicates that you are poised to live your life, at least for a while, in both the conscious and unconscious realms. This adaptability doubles your skills for achieving success in your endeavors. In a dream the frog may indicate transformation within you.

Fruit

There is a potential sexual connotation of fruit in a dream. In addition, fruit can be seen as the result of cultivation, either literal or metaphorical. It suggests the mature stage in a process as it nears completion.

Gander (see Duck)

Garden

Here we bring order to nature. The garden symbolizes the impact of intellect on one's surroundings. The trees, shrubs and flowers have their individual importance to you, as well as the placement of the paths, stones, or other features. How does this garden reflect the organization of your own conscious mind?

Gargoyle

In church architecture the gargoyle always takes a place lower than the angels. It symbolizes the demonic side of spirit. In a dream a gargoyle indicates the instinctual level of mind, or of a confusion of elements.

Garland (Lei)

Two principal meanings are possible for the garland: First, the garland, like any continuous figure, suggests the circle or mandala, a symbol of completeness. Second, it suggests a bond between different things (the individual flowers), and thus represents multiplicity. You may find that at first one of these definitions seems to fit your dream image, and then later you see the relevance of the other possibility.

Garuda

This fabulous bird is an attribute of the Hindu god Vishnu. It is eagle-like and holds a serpent in its claws. It symbolizes mastery over both fire and water.

GAZELLE

The gazelle symbolizes the soul (Cirlot 1971, 115). It bounds through life gracefully, yet is subject to the predator (instinctual behavior). In a dream the gazelle lightens the seriousness of life and at the same time elevates it, showing that the soul is life and that life serves the soul.

GEMINI

The third sign of the zodiac is represented by twins. It symbolizes the closeness of two things that are nearly identical, and at the same time different. In a dream this sign symbolizes a link between you and another dream figure, or a connection between two apparently different thoughts, feelings, or events. An example is the metamorphosis from caterpillar to butterfly.

GEMS (*see* JEWELS)

GENITALIA (PENIS, VAGINA, WOMB)

While Freud found sexual implications in all containers and phallic shapes, the converse is also true. A graphic depiction of the penis, for example, may relate more strongly to an individual's sense of self-importance and power. Whether you are male or female, the penis and your relation to it symbolize personal will and power. It is a special kind of magic wand. The vagina symbolizes both the capacity to contain and the ability to produce life. It is both an entrance to and an exit from the womb, a symbol of the beginning of life of beings, feelings, and ideas. For some people, graphic sexual dreams are disturbing and overly erotic in content. Such dreams may indicate that the conscious relationship to sexuality is restrictive or clouded in some way.

GIANT (*see also* TITANS)

Because the unconscious can exaggerate a feeling, a giant symbolizes something that is important for you to hear. The unconscious makes it large to make it more visible. What is the giant saying to you? What is it doing?

GIRAFFE

The giraffe is farsighted, due to its perspective so far above the ground. In alchemy the ability to rise above the details of ordinary life to see the overall picture is essential to personal growth, and the giraffe may be signaling that it is time to take just such a view of your life.

GLANCE (LOOK, STARE)

To glance is to understand everything with one look. Dream characters often suggest that they understand the drama in which they are participating, even when you don't grasp the meaning. A longer look suggests awareness and points to something of significance. A staring dream figure may have a hypnotic effect on you and draw you into the feeling of the stare; through the dream figure's hypnosis you may also intuit the focus of the stare.

GLOBE

The globe or sphere is a symbol of perfection and completeness.

GLOVES

Gloves symbolize dexterity, as does the hand. The quality of the glove suggests its significance—a baseball glove, for instance, is different from chain mail, or delicate lace. What is your dream glove like?

GLUE (*see* PASTE)

GOAT

Goats eat almost anything, and therefore are thought to be less evolved than other animals. The mountain goat climbs high to places where no one else can. The goat is the symbol for the ambitious zodiacal sign Capricorn. It is sure-footed, strong, and able to reach the top (of the mountain, of one's career, etc.).

GOBLET (*see also* CUP)

The first symbolic meaning is connected to the container itself: The goblet is designed to hold something. The second meaning derives from what you see in the cup, and the contents become a significant focus. What do you see in the cup?

GOLD

In a dream a gold object symbolizes the most valuable quality. It is the color of the sun, of the metal gold, and of spirit. It points to the thing that, if you focus on it, will reveal something of central importance to you. It represents the purified substance that is the goal of alchemy, and therefore the goal of psychological and spiritual development. It also symbolizes the light of the sun and thus divine intelligence.

GOLDEN FLEECE

The sheep or lamb denotes innocence, and gold denotes perfection. Thus the golden fleece symbolizes the perfect innocence that we feel we have lost. In a dream it indicates that your innocence is not so far away, and that it has great value.

GONG (*see* BELL)

GOOSE (*see* DUCK)

GORDIAN KNOT (*see* **LABYRINTH**)

GORGE (*see* **CANYON**)

GORGON
A woman with a beautiful face and hideous snakes for hair, the gorgon symbolizes an unbearable juxtaposition of two or more things. In a dream it can indicate that you are coming closer to accepting a paradox that has been keeping you from making progress.

GRAFTING
Grafting is a method of making one thing grow from another. It is an unnatural intervention. This dream symbol indicates that you have connected things closely together that would not naturally be attached to each other. What in your life represents an attempt to bring things together that may better exist apart, or that seem different, but fit together well for you?

GRAIL
The grail symbolizes two things. The first is the quest. In a dream the grail symbolizes a quest for something that will complete your spiritual being. The second is the grail itself, which is a container for the blood of the redeemer, and thus symbolizes redemption. To find the grail in a dream is to identify personal redemption or sacrifice.

GRAPES
Grapes symbolize fertility and life. They produce wine, which is a Christian symbol of Jesus' sacrifice. As a drink of the gods, wine symbolizes divine wisdom.

GRAPHICS (*see* **CIRCLE, DISK, SQUARE**)

GRASSHOPPER (*see* **CRICKET**)

GRAY
Gray is made up of shades between white and black, and thus reflects the multiple layers of meaning within the object of this color. It can be dull or murky, but it also can be the color of choice when you wish to become balanced. It may symbolize an early stage of integration of opposite ideas, something that dreams often indicate and encourage.

GREAT MOTHER
The archetypal image of the Great Mother embodies the feminine and its qualities of fertility, nurturing, and spiritual mana. Carl Jung felt that this image symbolizes the objec-

tive truth to be found in nature. There is also a fearsome aspect to the Great Mother. The feminine can symbolize being entirely contained, as in the womb.

GREEN

Green reflects sensation. In the Buddhist system green reflects the capacity for effective action. Green is the color of the heart chakra. It is also the color of church vestments during Trinity season. Green reflects growth, and thus the earth. It may symbolize growth or new growth in a dream. Typical emotions associated with green are envy and jealousy.

GRIFFIN (GRYPHON)

The griffin is a fantastic animal with the head, wings, and talons of an eagle and the body of a lion. As such it combines the vision and alertness of the eagle with the physical power of the lion. The griffin symbolizes the sun and its energy. There is a certain paradox between the groundedness and power of the practical on the one hand, and the vision and flight of the spirit on the other.

GROTESQUENESS

Any grotesque image symbolizes the union of the natural and unnatural, or the transition from one to the other. In a dream grotesque images suggest movement, as from fear to understanding.

GROUP (see FLOCK)

GROUSE (PEACOCK, QUAIL) (see also PHEASANT)

The peacock, quail, and grouse are related birds that thrive in the wild. Each has its own defined mating ritual: the peacock fans its showy tail, the grouse has a mating dance, and the quail has a vigorous mating ritual as well. All the birds of this family are associated with spring, birth, and new growth. When they appear in dreams they suggest that your emotions are more affected by one particular physical sense—the peacock means vision, the grouse means hearing, and the quail means touch.

GRYPHON (see GRIFFIN)

GUARDIAN

If a person is guarding something in a dream, the nature of the guardian suggests the emotional or spiritual reason for the guardianship. Any locked container or door suggests guardianship. What is being guarded or protected in your dream?

GUIDE (see SOPHIA)

GULL (SEAGULL)

The gull is associated with air and water and thrives on both. In dreams the gull reflects your personal relationship between the world of logical intellect—objectivity—and the world of the unconscious—hidden emotions. When soaring in the air, the gull may represent a clear perspective. When diving, and descent into the unknown is being depicted. This descent could feel reckless, or it may seem totally necessary and appropriate. When sitting on the surface of the water, the gull suggests a calmer, more relaxed intertwining of the intellect and the unknown.

GUN

Firearms have not existed long enough to gain archetypal significance, but they certainly are symbols of power in our culture. Freud gave guns sexual meaning. I feel force is the central theme. The weapon's appearance reveals the subtle nature of energy in the dream. Any target symbolizes the focus of power.

GUT (*see* BELLY)

$$\mathcal{H}$$

HAIR (*see also* BODY, CURL, HEAD)

Hair symbolizes the spirit; its color, length, and quality indicate the condition of spirit. Hair on the head symbolizes the higher expression of spirit, while body hair denotes a lower, instinctual expression. Because hair is hair whether it is on the head or body, it symbolizes the spirit within you. The American Indians used hair, particularly horsehair, to make fetishes to ward off negative energy and thus protect the owner.

HALF-LIGHT (*see* TWILIGHT)

HALLWAY (TUNNEL)

Halls and tunnels take you from one room to another, and from one dream scene to another. They symbolize spiritual, emotional, mental, or physical passages in your life. Thus a hallway may symbolize a transition in time or space. Is the transition a comfortable one? Does it seem positive (is there "light at the end of the tunnel")? Is it scary (very dark, perhaps)? Can you, when awake, actively imagine a safer, more secure passage?

HALO

In art, haloes are used to depict holy persons, angels, or deities. The halo's radiance suggests the capacity to express spiritual clarity.

HAMLET (*see* **LITERARY FIGURE**)

HAMMER

The hammer symbolizes both the creative power of forging metal or other construction, and the destructive power of smashing and breaking. Even if the hammer is used to break something in a dream, it incorporates the symbolism of creation. What is metaphorically being created in your dream?

HAND (**MUDRA**)

The hands provide a natural digital counting tool, and they provide the dexterity needed to make and use tools. They symbolize creative action in a dream. A particular gesture may serve as a sign to others. For example, shaking hands is a gesture of mutual respect. The right hand suggests the logical intellect, while the left suggests a nonrational or intuitive function. Some hand positions (mudras) are used to invoke certain states of mind during meditation.

HANGED MAN

The Hanged Man in tarot is a complex symbol incorporating heaven and earth and the feeling these have been reversed. In a dream the Hanged Man symbolizes a reversal of life's direction, with the spiritual or mystical taking precedence in your daily life over more mundane, practical details.

HARE (**RABBIT**)

Peter Rabbit, the legend of the tortoise and the hare, and the rabbit of the Chinese zodiac demonstrate that we have many associations with this fertility symbol. The rabbit can provide us with food and its warm fur can protect us from the cold. Within days of birth baby rabbits can maintain their body temperature, and within one lunar cycle they can survive on their own. Their large ears provide a warning system against predators. The rabbit may reflect timidness, fertility, curiosity, utter stillness, or great speed in your dream, or possibly some combination of all these traits.

HARP

The harp, an instrument of the gods and angels, symbolizes a connection between ordinary material existence and the spiritual realm as its music serves to communicate between these realms.

HARPIES

These fabulously ugly and evil figures symbolize dynamic movement in the spiritual realm. While they are often depicted as evil, they are not inherently so.

HAT

The hat symbolizes intellect. Its shape, color, size, and condition indicate specific qualities of intellect. How does your dream hat reflect your own intellect?

HAWK (FALCON) (*see also* SPARROW HAWK)

The hawk is symbolic of the messenger, attentive to the message and alert to its surroundings. In your dream the hawk is delivering a creative message, and you will need your intuition to help you decipher it. The hawk is also a soul symbol. Perhaps your soul is trying to speak to you, and sends the hawk messenger. The sharp talons signify the keenness (importance) of the message.

HEAD (*see also* BODY, CURL, HAIR)

The head is associated with intellect to the extent that intelligence is connected with the brain. A head separated from its body may indicate that intellect has been separated from its connection to the natural, instinctual side of your nature. The head also relates to a less physical, more mental or spiritual side of your being. Are you focusing, or do you need to focus more, on mental activities in your daily life? Can you work to create balance between physical and mental activities?

HEADDRESS (*see also* CROWN)

Head decorations often symbolize status. American Indians used feathers to indicate status as a warrior. Queens and other royalty wear crowns and tiaras. Scarves and bandanas symbolize functionality or workmanlike qualities. The function of the headdress symbolizes the psychological or spiritual values of the dream image.

HEART

The heart symbolizes the center of something: the spiritual center, and also the psychological center.

HEARTH

The hearth of a fireplace symbolizes the warmth of a home and the feeling of love found there.

HEAT

Heat in a dream symbolizes the psychological process of alchemy in which the impurities of thought and feeling are burned off, leaving the pure spirit. Heat in a dream is often accompanied by a sense of shame or embarrassment. It represents the energy for creative expression of all kinds, and is not limited to sexual libido.

HEAVEN

In numerous traditions heaven is a realm of spiritual purity where animal desires are sublimated. In a dream it can also symbolize the more objective positions we achieve when we can see the bigger picture.

HECATE (*see also* DIANA)

Hecate is a symbol of the Terrible Mother. Often seen as the evil side of the feminine, the Terrible Mother rises to defend her young when they are in danger, and thus she symbolizes a fierce protective quality as well.

HEDGEHOG (*see* PORCUPINE)

HELIOS

Helios is a god who symbolizes the power of the sun and the seasons.

HELL (*see* JOURNEY INTO HELL)

HELMET

The helmet is a protection for the head, and thus symbolizes a container for thought, or the thought itself. A strange crest or decoration symbolizes an unusually active imagination.

HEMISPHERE

The hemisphere implies the entire sphere, yet symbolizes the feeling of being contained in one half of reality, or of focusing on one side to the exclusion of the other.

HERBS

Herbs in a dream symbolize the dynamic hidden forces of nature. It is important to identify the herb and discover its natural properties. Then those properties may be associated with other dream images. Healing properties of herbs symbolize healing that is needed, or that is taking place, within the psyche.

HERCULES

Hercules symbolizes the individual struggle to attain freedom or immortality.

HERD (*see* FLOCK)

HERMAPHRODITE

Any person or figure in a dream with both male and female characteristics symbolizes the union of opposites, sexually, intellectually, and spiritually. It suggests a maturing of intellect as it learns to tolerate paradoxes.

HERMIT

The Hermit of tarot symbolizes the role of the teacher. It can include the positive traits of tradition, study, and instruction, as well as less constructive traits of tedious lessons and emotionally distant relationships. What is the dream trying to teach you?

HERON

The heron symbolizes good fortune brought to you through your own efforts. It indicates self-reliance, careful planning, and a protective attitude toward whatever is most important to you. Herons nest in the same area year after year, and are generally long-lived. Thus this bird in your dreams is a symbol of stability. The heron is able to wade into deep water, a sign that you are able to delve into the depths of your unconscious to obtain nourishment.

HERRING

A red herring is a distraction from the central point. In a dream the herring may, by its strong odor, lead you away from an important dream element, so associations with a herring in a dream are where you should focus your attention.

HEXAGRAM (*see* STAR OF DAVID)

HIEROGLYPHICS

Egyptian hieroglyphics, or any writing in a language or script unknown to you, symbolizes a communication from the unconscious that is unintelligible to you. It suggests the need to consider the lettering, absorb the feeling of the dream, and gather understanding from it. As you pay attention, the meaning may reveal itself or you may have another dream in which the writing becomes intelligible.

HIEROPHANT (PRIEST)

The Hierophant tarot card symbolizes the structure of tradition, often seen as the pope, or other rulers of tradition. It also symbolizes regulation, and the manifestation of spiritual law.

HIGH PRIESTESS (PRIESTESS)

In tarot, the High Priestess is the second card of the Major Arcana and she sits between the pillars of justice and mercy. She conceals knowledge in the scroll on her lap. Perhaps she appears in your dream to indicate that hidden knowledge is about to become clear to you either in your dream or your waking life. She also symbolizes the paradoxical inclusion of will and substance in one being, as creation is the expression of her will.

HIPPOPOTAMUS

The hippopotamus is related to the horse (*hippos* means horse in Greek) but the two are so very different in form and function. The hippopotamus is as much at home beneath the surface of water as the horse is on land. The hippopotamus is a massive animal symbolic of strength—the strength you can obtain from the less conscious parts of your psyche.

HOG (BOAR) (*see also* PIG)

Often thought as unclean animals, and in some cases known to carry disease, the hog is a highly intelligent animal, relatively close to human beings on the genetic scale. You may want to consider what bit of wisdom the pig brings you in your dream.

HOLE

The hole symbolizes a passage from one thing or place to another. The sexual meaning is only one possibility. It can indicate a passage into a different spiritual existence, and often indicates the path from life to death, or vice versa.

HONEY

Honey symbolizes wisdom. It also symbolizes the result of work, specifically the result of psychological or spiritual work.

HOOD

The hood is a symbol for the protection or hiding of the psyche or spirit. It suggests the invisibility of an idea or personal invisibility.

HORNS

There are several levels of symbolism where horns are involved. First, the horned shape, reminiscent of the crescent, symbolizes the hidden, spiritual side of life. Second, horns symbolize the fertility of a bull or the horn of plenty. Third, horns symbolize the capacity to extend one's voice through an amplification instrument, and therefore may indicate the amplification of a previous dream image.

HORSE

Speed and power are the essence of the horse (hence the term *horsepower* in reference to an automobile engine). There is also an element of escape in the speed. Although horses have been bred and supposedly domesticated, the horse is no docile pet. In a dream horses symbolize instinct and emotions of great power. They can represent sexual drives as well. White and black horses together symbolize opposites, such as life and death. The horse has a magical quality, and the horseshoe symbolizes good luck.

HOURGLASS

The hourglass first represents the passage of time. It also represents the potential for situations to get turned upside down. In a dream an hourglass can indicate something that has already happened, something that is happening (the present moment), or something that will happen (the future).

HOUSE

Houses in dreams symbolize the dreamer's entire being. The nature and shape of windows, doors, and rooms suggest the state of the psyche and its general organization and tidiness. Some say the windows symbolize the eyes, and the door symbolizes the mouth. The foundation suggests your feelings of stability in waking life at the time of the dream. The flow of air through the house may indicate the movement of thought, while water images suggest movement in the unconscious. Fire suggests intuition, and floors and their coverings suggest the practical foundation of the mind. When analyzing a part of a house in a dream, you will want to consider its color, quality, state of repair, and suitability to the dream situation. If the image is one you recognize, the meaning may be evident. If it is not one you recognize, or if it is distorted, then seek meaning in its unusual character. For example, stairs may seem ordinary enough at first, but they may become steeper and more difficult as you ascend or descend. This would suggest that the dream situation makes it difficult for you to become more objective (ascending), or more difficult to delve into unconscious material (descending).

HUMMINGBIRD

The hummingbird is a work of contradiction. It can fly in any direction, or hover in one spot. It uses large amounts of energy, but can nearly reach a hibernation state when at rest. It migrates over thousands of miles each year. People put out special feeders just so they can see this tiny delightful bird. Take joy from the hummingbird in your dream, and incorporate similar activities into your daily life.

HURRICANE (CYCLONE, TORNADO, WHIRLPOOL, WHIRLWIND) (*see also* BREEZE, WIND)

The hurricane, tornado, cyclone, whirlpool, and whirlwind have similar spinning motions, thrusts in the vertical plane, and potential for lateral movement. They symbolize the turbulent disturbance of one element (water or air), and the powerful effect it has on other elements. They also symbolize the strong psychic movement of ideas and feelings, without regard for the normal state of affairs. They may indicate a need for rapid change which will inevitably have a temporary disruptive effect.

IBIS

The ibis is an ancient Egyptian symbol of wisdom.

ICE

Ice is the solid form of water. Thus it symbolizes feelings that have hardened, or solidi-fied. This can mean that feelings have become cold or distant. It can also mean that feel-ings are moving into the practical realm and that you are ready to take action on deci-sions which have become clear.

IMPOSSIBILITY

An obstacle that feels impossible to overcome or a condition that seems impossible within the dream both indicate a dream sequence in which you have reached the edge of your objective understanding. It is important to discover possibility hidden in apparent impossibility, or to extend your understanding. By analyzing the various elements of such a dream, you extend your intuitive and intellectual grasp of the dream.

INCEST

Dreams concerning incest are some of the most powerful dreams we have. They may have the literal meaning of a sexual union with a family member. However, that is not the only symbolic meaning. There may also be a longing to merge with parts of one's own psyche that are depicted and understood as being similar, yet are different in some way. The incest symbology conveniently expresses this paradox, as it implies both same-ness and separateness. Incest is a powerful symbol for individuation.

INDIGO

Indigo is the color of the crown chakra.

INSECTS

We often think of insects as pests. They sting us, eat our crops, and invade our kitchens and homes. Yet they can show us something about our habits as we examine theirs. The single most apparent difference between insects and humans is their capacity for meta-morphosis. If the insect in your dream is in the larval state, then you become aware of the early development of important ideas or feelings within yourself. If the insect is devour-ing everything in sight, then you are in a healthy, growing stage of development. If the insect is buzzing about, look for busy elements in your own daily life. It is important to recognize that dramatic change is possible—and good.

INSTRUMENTS
A musical, surgical, artistic, or other instrument carries two meanings: The fact of which instrument it is is one. The other is its symbolic significance in the context of the dream. For example, a knife, by its shape and size, has a particular use in the material world. In the psychic realm, however, it may symbolize cutting through a specific kind of psychic or spiritual barrier.

INTERSECTION
An intersection symbolizes a point of decision or a choice. In dreams intersections suggest a transcendent direction.

INTESTINES
Being the part of the body where digestion occurs, the intestines may symbolize all that is welcomed or feared in the alchemical process.

INVERSION (AMBIVALENCE, CONTRAST, PARADOX) (see also ENIGMA)
Inversion occurs when one thing is changed into its opposite. Because the opposites are part of one process, they are not actually polar in nature, but in waking life they are experienced that way. An example is a dream in which beautiful sunny weather changes to a thunderstorm, or a spotless white dress becomes muddied, or vice versa. When you experience opposites in a dream, you are at the point where transcendence can occur.

INVISIBILITY
Invisibility suggests the symbolic repression of a feeling or idea that is too painful to keep in consciousness. It also may be a symbol for the dissolving of something that no longer has to exist in your consciousness.

IRON
Iron is used to make tougher, more durable steel—material that feeds industrial development. In a dream it may represent the changing of ages for you psychically. It also symbolizes the strength of the planet Mars, the astrological sign for exploration and independence. Iron is a key component of healthy blood, so iron in a dream may symbolize either the need for healthy habits or the fact that you are in a state of good health. Also, pressing a heated iron to fabric removes wrinkles. The heat may also kill bacteria in the fabric, thus purifying the cloth. In a dream the pressing, or urgent quality of the dream activity may be significant.

IRIDESCENCE

Mother-of-pearl or opals are iridescent. Iridescence may indicate the power of psychic sight. It also reflects the otherworldliness of angels and other beings.

ISLAND

An island symbolizes the point of contact between the conscious (air) and the unconscious (water). It also symbolizes isolation.

IVY

Ivy symbolizes several things: (1) immortality due to its ability to grow for lifetimes and propagate from a cutting, (2) the closeness and faith of friendship, and (3) the need for protection (because of its clinging nature).

JADE

Jade symbolizes immortality. What the jade object represents reveals the quality of immortality in your dream.

JAGUAR (COUGAR, LEOPARD) (*see also* CAT, LION, MOUNTAIN LION)

The jaguar is highly significant in Central American cultures, just as the leopard is in other parts of the world. These cats symbolize many manifestations of power. They inhabit many areas and can adapt to the terrain, and are even comfortable in water. They can respond with anger. In a dream the jaguar or leopard can represent anger or other intense emotions, instinctual responses, and raw power. They speak to a primal sort of power that can be mobilized to accomplish your waking goals.

JANUS

A two-faced image symbolizes the capacity to look forward and backward at the same time, and thus is a symbol of wholeness.

JESTER

The jester is a representation of the Trickster archetype. It appears in dreams to remind you that there is a serious and a humorous side to everything. On the psychic level the jester symbolizes the capacity for change and movement toward transcendence.

JEWELRY

In general a jewel symbolizes spiritual value. Fearsome animals, like dragons, protect such jewels. Jewelry adorns an individual. The tiara is a sort of crown and indicates the social or spiritual preeminence of the wearer. The earring focuses on hearing, and suggests paying special attention to what is said in the dream. Bracelets symbolize one's spiritual power by the stones and metals in the bracelet. Rings and bracelets indicate cycles of time, without beginning or end, and thus are often used in marriage ceremonies to represent fidelity. Depending on which finger the ring is on, a specific part of your nature is either being controlled (left hand) or expressed (right hand). The symbolism of a pin or brooch lies directly in the metal, gems, and the shape of the piece. Thus a butterfly pin has the symbolism of the butterfly first, and the metal and gems second. The same is true for a tie clip or tack.

JEWELS (GEMS)

Any jewel symbolizes a spiritual truth. Different gems have different meanings based on their chemical properties, color, and shape.

JOURNEY (TRAVEL, TRIP)

A journey symbolizes the desire for discovery that lies within your personality. The nature of the journey suggests the quality of the path you are pursuing.

JOURNEY INTO HELL (HELL)

Like Dante, your dream journey into hell is a descent into the darker, forbidden reaches of the psyche—the unconscious.

JUDGMENT

The Judgment card in tarot symbolizes the transition from one state of consciousness to another, or the transition from one state of understanding to another. It symbolizes illumination, healing, and resurrection.

JUICE

Juice symbolizes a life-giving property. In a dream you will want to drink the juice, as it is an offering of a life principle from the unconscious.

JUPITER

The planet Jupiter symbolizes great size, and also inflation (note: Jupiter is far less dense than Earth). The god Jupiter symbolizes judgment and will, and incorporates the qualities of wisdom and love into one being.

JUSTICE

The tarot image of Justice, with her scales, symbolizes the balance in your life. Justice refers to an inner sense of rightness and the psychic mechanism that gets you on the right path and maintains your course on it. This tarot card symbolizes firmness in intention. It sometimes indicates restriction or pettiness as well.

KACHINA

Kachinas are representations of the ancestral spirits of the Hopi and Zuni people. Each kachina symbolizes or personifies a specific type of spirit.

KANGAROO

The kangaroo and other marsupials approach life very differently. Their babies, tiny beings totally incapable of survival on their own, nest in the mother's pouch for the first part of their life. People in different cultures emulate the marsupial and use fabric to wrap their infants in carrying pouches. It is believed that babies carried close to the adult's heart are more content. The kangaroo is powerful and able to defend itself well. Thus the kangaroo symbolizes the security and protection we needed as children, and continue to require from time to time as adults.

KEYS

Keys symbolize a solution to a problem. In your dream a key may indicate that this dream contains a solution, or it may indicate where to look for the solution (behind a locked door, for example).

KING (*see also* QUEEN)

Royalty symbolizes something you feel ranks superior. If you find yourself in a dream with royalty, it may indicate that you feel your position in life is improving, or that you deserve equal status. If the king or queen has a particular quality in the dream, you may want to consider how that quality represents you at the time of the dream.

KING ARTHUR

King Arthur, a literary hero, embodies both the greatness and the smallness of human character. In addition, Arthur represents the promise of rebirth or resurrection, as he is expected to return again. His Knights of the Round Table reflect the twelve signs of the zodiac and Jesus' apostles.

KITCHEN

The kitchen and the act of cooking symbolize nurturing. The feeling of the room or the experience in the dream is significant. How do you feel about being there? Are you cooking up something for yourself or for someone else?

KNIFE (SHARP) (*see also* AXES, SWORD)

The knife symbolizes many things: As a man-made tool it represents intellect; as a weapon it symbolizes power or it may indicate a dangerous situation. The type of knife indicates the area of one's life or one's feelings that are most significant. The knife also represents the action of cutting through something.

KNIGHT

The knight symbolizes the spirit that has dominated the material world. If the Trickster is at play, then the knight appears to indicate that your dream is occurring at night, or that nighttime is significant to the dream in some way.

KNOT (LOOP) (*see also* CURL)

The knot symbolizes a link between two things. Because of its binding capacity, the knot is magical. Within the loops and knots of a net you may find anything from an old boot to fish to a monster. The weaving of knots is reminiscent of the labyrinth. In Buddhism the endless knot symbolizes good fortune, whereas the Gordian knot represents an insoluble puzzle. To undo a knot, to trace its path successfully, or to solve the mystery of the labyrinth, is to find one's center. A square knot is set firmly and will not slip when pressure is applied to the rope. A knot tied as a bow will slip loose when the end is pulled. Thus the bow exists only because no force is applied, and represents a relationship of trust. The knot symbolizes both binding (limitation) and linkage between things.

LABYRINTH (ARABESQUE, CELTIC KNOT, GORDIAN KNOT, MAZE)

The labyrinth, whether a pattern in floor tile or a garden with high hedges, is an apparently aimless set of paths that eventually lead to a center, or the core of one's being. In a dream a labyrinth suggests that you are on the path to discovering your center. In many cases, a maze is more easily solved by beginning at the end, and this paradox in a dream may point to another paradox, or problem, you are trying to solve. The center symbolizes a solution. When your dream includes one of these patterns, it indicates the complexity of a problem or a situation you are experiencing, either in your waking life on in your psychic life. The more complex the pattern, the more factors that may be involved, or the more intense the lost feeling you may have. You can choose to cut through the knot with an arbitrary solution, or you can choose to allow it to unravel, revealing the multitude of factors involved.

Ladder (*see* Stairs, Steps)

Lake

A lake symbolizes the mystery of the unconscious mind and its relationship to consciousness. It also brings together the elements of air and water in a single image and symbolizes both the intuition and the intellect as part of one whole.

Lamb

Innocence is the quality most often associated with the lamb. The lamb also symbolizes the perpetual renewal of life, as we repeatedly shear a lamb or sheep to obtain its wool.

Lamp (Lantern)

The lamp symbolizes the light of spirit, and also the light of intelligence. Aladdin's lamp contained a genie who could perform great feats. Any lamp suggests the power of creative thought and action. The Hermit tarot card incorporates a lantern into its symbolism to represent illumination which arises from diligent effort.

Lance

The lance is a weapon, and in a dream it symbolizes the power of taking the direct path. It may be a phallic symbol, but should not be limited to that meaning, as the direct path often has no sexual undertone.

Lantern (*see* Lamp)

Lapis

Lapis is the substance that remains after an alchemical process of purification is complete. The lapis stone is clear blue, sometimes flecked with gold. With reference to psychological work, lapis in a dream represents what remains to the self when impurities (misunderstandings) have been removed (clarified). In both the East and the West the stone is associated with introspection and inner work. The stone is thought to enhance psychic powers.

Lark (*see* Meadowlark)

Latch (*see* Bolt)

LEAD

A lead object symbolizes the base material from which gold can be made in alchemy. Psychologically lead translates to a basic state of mind from which you have moved in your journey toward wholeness.

LEAF

When leaves appear in your dream, consider both their shape and the plant from which they came, as they are significant to you. It is possible that leaves may symbolize people in your life, or periods of time (related to the seasons of the year or the pages of a book).

LEG

The condition of a leg in your dream may relate to your ability to move within the dream situation. For example, a well-formed limb suggests the capacity for graceful decision-making and action.

LEI (*see* GARLAND)

LEO

This sign of the zodiac is associated with royalty, and symbolizes your will, intuitive power, and the tempering process associated with fire, as in hardening steel, baking bread, or firing pottery.

LEOPARD (*see* CAT, JAGUAR, LION, MOUNTAIN LION)

LETTERS (ALPHABET)

Letters have the significance of language, through their shape and sound. In addition, they may symbolize any object, animal, or being associated with the letter. Lastly, the shape of the letter may be associated with a particular place, facial feature, or other object (e.g., a "T" on a road sign indicates the type of intersection ahead).

LEVEL

The relative level of things in your dream relates to the psychic or spiritual level. The lower level (basement, underground) is the unconscious or instinctual level, while higher floors in buildings and other high spots relate to the objective level of conscious mind or the higher spiritual planes.

LEVIATHAN (LOCH NESS MONSTER, SEA DRAGON)

A monstrous water entity symbolizes the power of the unconscious mind and its contents. There is an emotional charge to the symbol since the content is unfamiliar. Because we cannot survive underwater, fear of drowning is often associated with images of a leviathan. However, its appearance in a dream is a signal that you are in close contact with your emotions, and that clearer understanding is at hand. As you examine the details of the water monster, you will begin to understand the feeling of the message in your dream.

LIBRA

The seventh sign of the zodiac is associated with balance. It is the time when summer and winter are balanced—day and night are equally long. Libra symbolizes psychic balance as well. Astrologically it is associated with relationships, with the balance of justice, and with the kidneys.

LIGHT

Light is a symbol for spirit. Turning on a light implies an infusion of spirit into a dream scene. Light is also a creative cosmic force, and the particular creative quality can be described by its color and intensity.

LIGHTNESS

There are three types of lightness: relating to sound, vision, and weight. The sensation of any one of these in a dream can symbolize the others. Thus the feel of thin cotton fabric suggests of soft music or pastel colors. Any such dream objects and sensations suggest the capacity to become objective, or the movement between objectivity and concrete practicality. The fine fabric can stand in for a phrase like, "lighten up," or "I see the light (I understand)".

LILITH

Lilith embodies the threatening dark side of the feminine. In a dream this figure may represent something you do not wish to face, either from your past or in general. The dark feminine figure relates, not to the mother herself, but to feelings associated with her. Fear is certainly one of these, and power is another. As you examine this dream figure, consider which of her characteristics you can identify within yourself. If she has sharp teeth or long fingernails, how do you feel about them? How can you take the best of that power and apply it creatively?

LILY

The lily is symbolic of the Virgin Mary, and by association, of purity. The lily's blossom grows out of the mire, and symbolizes the potential for pure spirit to arise from any base condition. The lily has been a symbol of royalty, and therefore suggests the idea that purity of spirit is worth seeking.

LINE

The straight line is the core of geometric principles, yet there is no such thing in nature. The line is a direct path from one point to another. It can also divide two things, or represent the edge of an object. A horizontal line symbolizes the horizon, even though the actual horizon curves. It thus suggests a larger world outside the self. In astrology the horizontal line connects the individual personality of the ascendant with the outer world (descendant). The vertical line represents the individual being—the "I." It suggests the link between conscious and unconscious aspects of the mind. In astrology the vertical line connects the deepest well of the inner mind (nadir) to public expression and ego consciousness (midheaven).

LINGAM

The lingam is a stylized phallus symbolic of the Hindu god Shiva. A symbol for the integration of the sexes, the lingam symbolizes the creative power of the universe. An object of this shape in a dream reflects your own creative capacity. The feminine counterpart to the lingam is the yoni.

LION (COUGAR, LEOPARD) (*see also* CAT, JAGUAR, MOUNTAIN LION)

The lion is often thought of as the king of beasts, yet this cat has tremendous feminine power. It is the female who hunts and raises the cubs. The lion symbolizes a supreme position of power and does not need to fight for survival. It approaches its quarry silently and stealthily. The lion never needs to lie, as the truth is one facet of its strength. If the Trickster is involved in your dream, the lion can symbolize pride and may be cautioning you to assess your position carefully and not underestimate your potential.

LITERARY FIGURE (HAMLET)

Hamlet, or any literary figure in a dream, symbolizes the quality inherent in the character. Hamlet embodied the anguish of indecision. What is the essential quality you associate with the literary figure in your dream?

LIZARD

Lizards are quick and have highly adapted senses of hearing, smell, and sensitivity to vibration. In a dream they may symbolize heightened awareness, a quality that pertains to many dreams. If there is a prominent facet of the lizard's physical appearance, its special significance should be considered. The pattern of skin coloring, the length of the body or tail, and the direction of movement can all reveal important dream messages. Consider how you feel about the lizard and its appearance.

LOAVES

Loaves of bread symbolize the fruitful harvest. They share the symbolism of sexual fruitfulness as well.

LOCH NESS MONSTER (*see* **LEVIATHAN**)

LOCK (*see* **BOLT**)

LOCUSTS

Locusts were one of the plagues in the Bible sent to torment the Egyptians, and they also appear in the Book of Revelation. They came in waves and ate everything in their path. Perhaps their most compelling quality is relentlessness. Are you experiencing something relentless in your waking life?

LOGOS

A dream figure associated with the Logos has the qualities of light and life. It is therefore symbolic of both life-giving physical properties and the creative capacity of intellect. It has the capacity of spirit to dispel darkness and disorder, and is the antithesis of chaos.

LOOK (*see* **GLANCE**)

LOOP (*see* **CURL**, **KNOT**)

LORELEI (**MERMAID**) (*see also* **SIREN**)

Generally feminine, the siren produces an irresistible song that lures sailors off course and into the rocks or reefs. The Lorelei symbolizes temptation. How do you relate this symbol of temptation to the dream or to your waking life?

LOSS (**LOST**)

Ranging from misplaced objects, to the loss of a loved one, to the loss of a contest or race, it is the feeling of loss that has taken tangible form in the dream. While the loss feels much like death, finding an object, a loved one's return, or rematch on the playing field are all symbolic of resurrection or rebirth. The two are inseparable; "lost" in a dream merely precedes "found."

LOST (*see* **LOSS**)

LOTUS (**ROSE**)

The lotus and rose share symbolic meaning in Eastern and Western cultures. Both share the form of the mandala, a circle with a center, and thus both symbolize the heart, particularly the spiritual heart. But where the lotus symbolizes emanation of life from the spiritual center in the East, the rose's spiritual center is more often seen as hidden in the West. The physiology of the flowers reveal this difference, too. Also, the number of petals in the flower may be significant.

LOVED ONE

Generally a feminine entity, the loved one as a symbol probably originated in Persia. Whether male or female, the loved one may symbolize the experience of human love, or it may relate to the spiritual devotion at the root of many mystical religious practices.

LOVER

The Lover in tarot is faced with two choices: one is viewed as morally and intellectually proper, the other is seen as lewd or base. The choice between these two symbolizes all choices that present a dilemma. If you are faced with such a choice in your dream, you may want to examine the options, not as two opposite possibilities, but as two parts of a third, synthetic possibility.

LYNX

The lynx is secretive. In a dream it suggests you have the capacity to seek out the secrets of your environment, your unconscious, and the spiritual realm. The lynx promises that there is more to be known. The idea is to bring secrets out into the light so you can examine them and learn from them. Yet the lynx does not seek out information for no reason. Thus its actions in your dream may indicate the nature of your curiosity and its best potential direction at the time of the dream.

LYRE

The lyre, a seven-stringed musical instrument, symbolizes the harmony of the planets, which in turn symbolize the Solar Mind—the intelligence of our solar system as a whole—or Logos. The lyre, a physical instrument, symbolizes the link between the physical and the heavenly.

MACE

Traditionally the mace was either a staff of office or a weapon with a spiked ball at the top. The spice mace comes from the outer covering of nutmeg. Mace is also a chemical spray used to immobilize an attacker. Mace often symbolizes the destruction of the subjective world in favor of the intellect.

MACHINE

A machine symbolizes human function in your dream. The nature of the machine and its condition reveals something about yourself. A flat tire on a car, for example, could indicate an injury to your foot, or a lack of understanding of something.

Macrocosm (Void) (*see also* Abyss, Emptiness, Nothingness, Space)

The macrocosm is the larger celestial system that includes spirit—the universe. The Void has two basic meanings: in Western religion the universe was created out of the Void, whereas in Eastern thought the Void coexists with creation. Within your psyche, the Void, or empty space, may be perceived as an abyss with frightening characteristics. However, it is within this spaciousness that the creative process begins. Therefore, when such a symbol appears in a dream, it indicates that the creative juices are flowing, even if you don't have anything tangible to show for them.

Magician (*see also* Trickster)

In tarot, the Magician is the first card of the Major Arcana and is capable of using the elements to create infinite diversity. He is also capable of using those same elements to trick us into understanding things that have eluded us because of our own capacity to ignore the obvious.

Maize (Corn)

Maize, or corn, is symbolic of prosperity and fertility.

Major Arcana (*see* Tarot)

Malformation (Distortion)

Physical distortions or ailments in dreams can relate directly to a weakness in one part of the dreamer's body. Distortion could symbolize a weak or distorted quality of character. It may also indicate that you have been carrying a metaphoric burden that has caused stress to your body, or that your work is causing physical injury. Thus to dream of a foot injury may indicate actual problems, it may relate more to your understanding of situations, or it may indicate a need to finding the proper fit for yourself in a situation. Physical symptoms are often the result of long-standing effort or weakness on emotional and spiritual levels, and the dream may simply be showing you how your activities in waking life are playing out on the emotional or spiritual planes.

Mandala (*see also* Belt, Bicycle)

The simplest mandala is a circle, with its center shown or implied. This is a profound symbol of wholeness. In Eastern traditions this *yantra,* or image, is used as a focus for meditation and concentration. Many mandalic images incorporate triangles or squares, and each represents something about the mind of its author. Psychically the mandala represents order. Mandalas appear in dreams to provide a sense of order within the personality. The mandala is one of the oldest known symbols as it was found in art from the Paleolithic Age, and yet it endures to modern times in art, in games, and in imagination.

Mark (*see* Brand)

MARRIAGE

A dream marriage is the union of two people, and thus symbolizes the union of opposite forces within your personality. The circumstances of the marriage may reveal what those forces are.

MARS

A fiery red planet and a Roman god, Mars symbolizes energy at work. This planet is associated with agricultural creativity, blood flow, and the surgeon and his skills. It also symbolizes both war and the warrior.

MARSH (BOG, FEN, SWAMP)

Decomposition is a primary feature of low, wet ground. A marsh may symbolize a lack of fire or air energy within your dream experience. At the same time it symbolizes the fertility of earth and water. The marsh also symbolizes the feeling of being bogged down in a project that has little or no forward movement. While the focus is on lack of movement, the symbol implies growth potential.

MARTIN (see SWALLOW)

MASCULINE

Masculine figures in dreams are who they are, but they also may symbolize the archetypal masculine—Youth, Father, Hero, Wise Old Man. Does your dream figure stimulate ideas or feelings about the masculine side of your character? your life?

MASK (see DISGUISE)

MATRON

An older female figure suggests the domineering quality of the mother. When you go beyond that surface quality, you see the wisdom gained through life experience.

MAYA

In Hindu belief *maya* is the illusion in which we live as physical beings. It is only vaguely related to spiritual reality, and we comprehend spirit through the veil of this illusion. The Maya of Central America are a race of Indians whose ancient civilization was highly structured. The Hindu culture focused on solar and lunar cycles of time, while the Central American culture focused on the cycles of the planet Venus.

MAZE (see LABYRINTH)

MEADOW

The meadow symbolizes openness and freshness in that there are no trees. Psychically the meadow is generally felt to be a safe place for the very reason that there are no trees among which dangers may lurk.

MEADOWLARK (LARK)

The meadowlark is a symbol of a cheerful attitude toward life. In a dream it can indicate that whatever action is taking place is associated with fun in some way.

MEPHISTOPHELES

Mephistopheles symbolizes the negative, destructive, psychic function. The more independent this dream figure is, the more out of control you may feel your life is.

MERCURY

This winged messenger symbolizes communication of all kinds. In a dream he may be the messenger, or he may symbolize that this dream imparts a message. The metallic element mercury is liquid at room temperature, and thus has the property of freedom of movement associated with the god.

MERMAID (see LORELEI, SIREN)

METALS

In general metals represent qualities within consciousness. A base metal such as lead represents a base or primitive psychic force, while a pure metal (pure in this sense indicating higher spiritual purity) such as gold symbolizes a transmutation of the base and a liberation from traditional limitations of the psyche. Metals also represent both the creativity and the constraints of civilization.

METAMORPHOSIS (TRANSFORMATION, TRANSMUTATION)

A metamorphosis is a total change—one thing becomes another. Such a change in a dream symbolizes the global changes you may be experiencing in some area of your life. This kind of transformation is nearly always seen as positive (compare the fuzzy, somewhat creepy quality of a caterpillar to the beautiful brilliance of the butterfly).

MICE (see MOUSE)

MICROCOSM

Man, the individual, is the microcosm. Within our physical, mental, emotional, and spiritual experience is reflected everything in the universe, and vice versa.

MINARET

The call to prayer goes out from the minaret and symbolizes the potential connection between the mundane and the spiritual sides of life.

MINK

The mink is a symbol of value. Because mink are at home on land and in water they symbolize an ability to understand your personal unconscious motivations.

MINOTAUR

Part bull and part man, the minotaur symbolizes a union between intelligence and powerful instincts. When it appears in a dream it indicates a situation that is larger than life or that is outside your normal circumstances.

MINSTREL (*see* FOOL)

MIRROR

A mirror in a dream can signal that you are about to enter a lucid dreaming phase. As you recognize yourself, you are able to take independent action within the dream. There is also the possibility of being contained within the mirror. Mirrors are magical instruments in which you may find distant scenarios. They are also used in *feng shui,* the Chinese study of environmental balance, to redirect energy flow.

MIST (FOG)

Mist in a dream conceals a dream element or suggests concealment of something else. It is a blending of air and water, and symbolizes the union of intuition and intellect in the reasoning process.

MISTLETOE

Mistletoe symbolizes regeneration, and thus fertility.

MONKEYS

Monkeys are lower primates and may seem less intelligent, but this is only because we don't understand their language. When a monkey appears in a dream, it alludes to copying others, which has its the benefits and drawbacks. Monkeys are clever, and may represent the Trickster archetype.

MONOLITH

A massive stone symbolizes a unified force that counterbalances the multiplicity of the material world. The stone focuses creative energy.

MONSTER

Monsters symbolize psychic contents that are fearful, primitive cosmic forces. They may represent an imbalance of psychic energy, or an unnatural juxtaposition of two or more things or ideas. The monster may symbolize what you believe is an uncontrollable feeling. While such a creature seems to pose a threat, it also has within it the power to achieve great things if you can harness its energy. You don't need to slay the dragon to do this. Rather, you may want to examine it, make friends with it, and tame it.

MOON

Lunar symbolism is so broad that you may want to find literary references to broaden the definition presented here. Even though the moon is much smaller and colder than the sun, we perceive it as the same size because of its relative distance from the Earth. Thus it is positioned as a psychic equal to the sun. Its cycle matches the menstrual cycle, and is thought to match many medical phenomena and life rhythm cycles. The moon symbolizes the night, the imagination, the potential for change, and the dream itself.

MOOSE

The call of the moose is like a bellow. A moose is very large, powerful, and potentially dangerous, but it can also be gentle. A symbol for long life, the moose in your dreams may suggest being attentive to elders, or that you are becoming an elder within your own social group.

MOTHER

Whether your own mother or a mother figure appears in your dreams, she symbolizes both the security and nurturance of childhood, as well as a devouring fierceness often associated with the feminine. She symbolizes flexibility of social principles, as in contrast with patriarchal rigidity.

MOUNTAIN

The mountain represents a spiritual height. Mount Fuji is seen as the spiritual center of the world for the Japanese, while Kilimanjaro is a similar center for Africa. An active volcano is a mountain that reveals its symbolic power through fire and smoke. The Himalayas reach the highest physical altitude and therefore reflect high spiritual aspirations. The mountain may also symbolize a large problem to be solved or a grand task to be accomplished. The Chinese associate the mountain with the protection and generosity of the emperor. Mountains are the source of warmth (coal) and wealth (precious metals). Examine the mountain in your dream to see which, if any, of these ideas are appropriate.

MOUNTAIN GOAT

Sure-footed, mountain goats climb high among the rocks, and seem to love the freedom of the heights. In a dream they can symbolize the capacity to seek out a higher vantage point—greater objectivity. They can also suggest the need to remain grounded and aware of one's surroundings.

MOUNTAIN LION (COUGAR, LEOPARD) (see also CAT, JAGUAR, LION)

Like any big cat, the mountain lion signifies a position of power, and therefore becomes a target for the envy of others. The dream image of the mountain lion suggests that you may have more innate power than you are aware of, and that you can cultivate this power. You have to stand by your convictions and hold your own ground when pushed by others.

MOUNTAIN SHEEP

Mountain sheep symbolize the capacity for survival in difficult terrain.

MOUSE (MICE)

The mouse has very short range vision, and must be close to an object in order to identify it. As a dream symbol the mouse may indicate that you need to pay attention to the details that are right in front of you, or it could mean that you are already lost among those details. The shortness of vision is both a strength and weakness. Its strength is to see the truth for what it is, without embellishments. The mouse indicates that organization is central to your life.

MOUTH

The mouth symbolizes creativity—the creative word. In your dream the mouth focuses attention on the translation of thought into word or action. On the other hand, the mouth may symbolize a devouring function. On the psychic level, the mouth serves both for intake of energy and its output.

MOVEMENT

Movement or limitation of movement in a dream forces you to focus. Movement indicates direction, for example, while speed indicates relative urgency. Lack of movement indicates that you need to stop to consider something you are not aware of.

MUD

Mud shares the creative symbolic potential of the marsh but generally does not incorporate the symbology of dissolution. Mud in a dream suggests the possibility of new growth. If you are stuck in it, it means that you may need to be patient.

MUDRA (see HAND)

MULTIPLICITY (see FLOCK)

MUSIC

Music presents a complex symbolism that can be explored far beyond a brief definition. It includes rhythm, melody, harmonics, and much more. As such it provides an avenue to the soul through the senses, yet sound also glorifies the human spirit. Consider the feeling the music in your dream evokes. Does it stimulate some intellectual activity, either within the dream, or as you record it?

Nakedness (*see* **Nudity**)

Names

Often you will immediately recognize the dream name. In this case you may decide to record information about the name and its known meaning(s). If you do not know the name, you may decide to look it up in the dictionary, encyclopedia, on the Internet, or check another reference source. A librarian may be able to help you if the word seems to be in another language.

Narcissus

Narcissus was a beautiful youth in Greek mythology who so admired his reflection in a pool that he was turned into a flower known today at the daffodil (narcissus). Both such a youth and the flower may indicate that you have turned much of your attention toward yourself, or that you need to pay more attention to yourself.

Nature

Natural scenes in dreams indicate locations for dream action and determine the flow of the dream by the ease or difficulty of the terrain. Natural scenes may also indicate that the dream calls for a more natural response to the dream situation. For example, if the scene includes a group of people around a boardroom table, but the table is in the forest, then you may need to take a more natural direction in your dealings with the group, instead of being overly formal or intellectual.

Necklace

Just as a necklace is composed of multiple beads, the image suggests the unification of multiple ideas or things. The color and quality of the beads are important to understanding the ideas or their connection to each other.

Neptune

The god of the sea, Neptune was once the god of the heavens and of fresh water as well. His descent into the sea suggests the vast body of the unconscious mind. When he appears in a dream, it may indicate that you are embarking on a journey into less conscious territory. He may serve as your guide if you invite him.

Net (Snare, Web)
(*see also* **Entanglement, Spider, Spider Woman, Spinning, Weaving**)
Any net, whether for hair or fishing, indicates searching the less conscious part of your mind. The net serves as a snare to hold your unconscious intelligence. Consider the contents of the net as it offers important information about your dream or yourself.

NIGHT

Often dreams about the night are in black and white, even if you normally dream in color. By the same token, a black-and-white dream may be interpreted as a nighttime dream, when in fact it is not. Once you have made this distinction, if the dream is about the night, this may indicate that you are acknowledging the value of sleep as a healing or informational resource. Consider how the dream action would be different if it occurred in the daylight.

NINE

Nine represents the body, intellect, and spirit manifested in three forms. It is a balanced number that reproduces itself—the result of multiplication by nine produces a number, the digits of which add to nine. When nine appears in a dream, there is a psychic connection to make. It indicates that you are in tune with your environment, your inner being, and your spirit.

NORTH

North is the direction of memory and the less conscious aspects of mind. Travelling there in a dream means you are seeking information from within yourself.

NOTHINGNESS (VOID) (*see also* ABYSS, EMPTINESS, MACROCOSM, SPACE)

Emptiness, the Void, and nothingness can be frightening in a dream. They may seem to indicate death or the state of being lost. However, the Void is more aptly the thing from which creation and creativity emerge. Nothingness can be eternal rest, or it can be the space in which you create your next good idea.

NUDITY (NAKEDNESS)

If you or other dream figures are nude, this indicates all pretense has been stripped away. Examine the dream closely to determine what it is showing you that you might not ordinarily consider. There may be a feeling that accompanies the nudity, and that feeling is an important one. It represents how you would feel if you could remove the intellectual trappings of your conscious mind to see what is underneath.

NUMBERS

Numbers have a quantitative value in dreams, but they also have metaphysical values. If the number is familiar, like your address or birth date, then it is a reference to that area of your life. When the number seems to stand on its own, write the number on a plain piece of paper and gaze at it, opening your mind to its message. You may also want to treat it as individual digits and look up each of their meanings.

Nymphs

Nymphs are mythical beings associated with flowing water in streams, rivers, fountains, and so on. When they appear in your dream, they call you to look into the less conscious part of your being, specifically the unconscious feminine component. This is possibly more true for males, but females will also find much to be gained by examining their unconscious femininity.

Oak

The oak symbolizes strength and long life. It is sometimes used to symbolize the mind—the branches being the conscious mind and the roots representing the unconscious portion of the psyche.

Oar

The oar is an instrument both for propulsion and for steering. Thus it symbolizes the power of intellect and the strength of will within each of us.

Obsidian

Obsidian is solid black volcanic glass which is formed from granite when subjected to the tremendous heat of volcanic activity. The glass will hold a sharp edge, although it is not as hard as the diamond. It symbolizes the grounding effect of all things that are solid. Any image reflected in its surface is of primary importance in the dream.

Ocean (Sea)

(*see also* Deluge, Rain, Rainbow, Reefs, River, Water, Wave, Wetness)

The ocean symbolizes the vastness and the diversity of the mind, with its visible waves and currents, and its less obvious depths and denizens. It also may symbolize the collective mind of all conscious beings.

Octagon

This shape is used for stop signs in the practical world, but in the dream context it symbolizes spiritual regeneration. So a stop sign in your dream will mean "stop," and also "stop so you can experience spiritual regeneration," or "stop to notice that you have undergone a spiritual regeneration."

OCTOPUS

The eight-tentacled octopus symbolizes the four cardinal and the four intermediary directions. It also is reminiscent of the spider's web, a symbol of the mystic center of creation.

OGRE

An ogre symbolizes the Terrible Father who eats his own children, like the gods Uranus and Saturn. In a dream an ogre symbolizes a thought pattern or idea that threatens to take over your conscious activities.

OLD AGE (see WISE)

OLD MAN

An old man symbolizes wisdom, and offers you something that you have not yet understood in your waking life. An old man also symbolizes the setting of the sun.

OLD THINGS (see ANTIQUES)

OLIVE TREE

The olive branch is a symbol of peace.

ONE

One symbolizes unity of being. Unity is a principal of action—your best activities occur when you are unified in your intention. Unity is a transcendent reality, and one is a singularity among variety.

OPOSSUM

An opossum dream image symbolizes the capacity to hide or become invisible to others. The Trickster is evident when the opossum appears as it shows you one thing while it suggests you look for deeper meaning. The opossum also appears to show you that appearances can mask reality, and that you have the capacity to appear larger than you are or different in some way.

ORANGE

Orange is the color of the navel chakra. It is also the color of the harvest season, and thus maturity.

ORCHESTRA

The orchestra, as a working unit, symbolizes the whole of your being. If one part of the orchestra dominates, it is a metaphor for some imbalance in your conscious life.

ORGY

Wild parties, drunkenness, and sexual excess are examples of orgiastic dream action. Chaos is the quality of the less conscious part of mind, and chaotic dream activity reflects disturbing or possibly destructive activity deep within you. Keep in mind that the dream does not regulate its depiction of a disturbance, so the dream action may be far more extreme than the conscious experience upon which it is commenting.

ORIOLE

The oriole symbolizes sunshine—the light, bright quality of summer—and hence a bright, happy spirit.

ORNAMENTATION

Any decorated object symbolizes relative order—the more refined the decoration, the more orderly the dream contents.

OSTRICH

An awkward bird, this animal is swift and powerful. It does not fly, and therefore its intelligence is of a practical nature. The second meaning of the ostrich—a person who avoids problems by denying their existence—should also be considered when this bird appears in a dream. The reality is that the ostrich knows when to protect itself by pulling its head down.

OTTER

The otter symbolizes playfulness and curiosity. They clearly enjoy playing in the water and the sun. The otter is also a symbol for the feminine, and the mother in particular, as the female otter is most attentive to her children. Consider your own playful, yet nurturing side.

OUROBOROS (SNAKE) (*see also* SERPENT)

The snake biting its own tail is symbolic of time and of continuity.

OVEN

An oven, like any container, symbolizes the feminine, specifically the womb and gestation.

OWL

The owl is a powerful animal, bringing with it clairvoyance (the owl has excellent long-range vision), magic (both black and white), and wisdom (the owl is the companion of Athena, the goddess of wisdom). The owl may indicate that you can hear or see what is in other people's hearts, and that you can identify truth. Owl and hawk feathers used together in a dream bundle may help you achieve a lucid dream state (Andrews 1993, 177). Being a nocturnal bird, the owl sometimes symbolizes death. Thus a dream owl may indicate a transformation in your life.

Ox (Cow) (*see also* Bull)

The ox is associated with aleph, the first letter of the Hebrew alphabet. As such it is symbolic of beginnings. The ox or bull is the second sign of the zodiac. At about the time when the symbols of the zodiac took on their names (4000–2000 B.C.), the sun rose in the constellation of Taurus at the spring equinox. Even though Taurus is now the second sign after the equinox, both the sign and the bull retain the symbolic nature of the early stages of the growth cycle. The bull and ox share qualities of patience and endurance, able to work long hours at a task. The ox or bull in your dream may also symbolize one of the four cardinal directions, the four elements, or the writers of the Gospels.

Palace

With its many rooms, a palace symbolizes a well-developed psyche. Located at the center of being, the palace represents organization within each of us that incorporates the mind and the heart together.

Palm

The palm tree is a symbol of victory (palm branches were laid in Jesus' path when he entered Jerusalem for the last time). The palm of the hand when held facing out is a signal to stop. It also contains the entire progress of one's life according to palmists. In a dream these meanings may be combined, hence indicating that victory is "at hand." A palm may also indicate something about your future life is being revealed.

Pan (*see also* Dionysus)

The god Pan is a symbol of nature and its potentially aggressive force. The kitchen utensil symbolizes the feminine, the domesticated, and the cultured side of human society.

Pandora

Pandora herself was not wicked, only curious. However, she turned loose the troubles we all face, according to the myth of her box. However, when she opened her box, she also released hope, without which we would be lost.

Pansy

This five-pointed flower symbolizes thought, and its deep color reflects the potential nobility of mind.

PAPYRUS

This early recording medium symbolizes the history of thought and communication, and therefore indicates that you are looking back into history for the ideas represented in your dream.

PARADISE

Paradise in a dream symbolizes the center of the psyche. An island paradise, for example, is in the center of the ocean of unconsciousness, and the Garden of Eden was located amidst external chaos. Paradise can be likened to the eye of a hurricane where there is a window of calm.

PARADOX (*see* ENIGMA, INVERSION)

PARAKEET

The parakeet is a messenger. In your dream it indicates that a message is being transmitted, perhaps from the personal unconscious or perhaps from the collective mind.

PARALYSIS

Any physical limitation in a dream may be related to an actual physical problem. Whether paralysis is a real possibility or not, a dream of paralysis symbolizes the feeling of limitation. Think of the rabbit that becomes completely still out of fear. Often the lack of movement symbolizes the dilemma of two very different choices in waking life. Are you facing such a decision? You may want to examine the choices, and then ask for another dream to help you decide which way to go. Paralysis in a dream may also indicate that you need to stop physical movement in order to focus on mental, emotional, or spiritual matters.

PARTRIDGE

For a bird that does not follow its mother when young, the partridge is often portrayed as perfidious and capable of deception or temptation in myths and stories. *The Partridge Family* television show detailed the lives of five children who all seemed to go their own way, and showed us that independence is a good trait to cultivate. In the Christmas song, the partridge in a pear tree is only one of many frivolous gifts one might receive.

PASTE (GLUE)

Paste and glue symbolize the capacity within the dream to bond things together. Some dreams bond unlike objects, and may remind us of the tenacity of a tar baby or of misapplied superglue. Consider how being bonded to the dream images feels—appropriate and useful, or distasteful and fearsome.

PATH (*see* **STAIRS, STEPS**)

PEACOCK (*see* **GROUSE, PHEASANT**)

PEARL

The pearl symbolizes the human soul, especially when there is only one in the dream. It also symbolizes heaven in many religions, or at least the qualities that will take us there.

PEE (*see* **URINE**)

PEGASUS

A mythical animal that resembles a horse with wings, the pegasus represents the capacity to soar to spiritual heights while living in a physical, earth-bound body. It may also symbolize the potential to transmute evil or limitation into good.

PELICAN

In religious symbolism the pelican symbolizes Christ. In alchemical literature, the pelican was said to feed its young from itself. Still, in a dream the pelican may refer to your nurturing capacity. The pelican is buoyant, so when it dives into the water to catch a fish, it can pop up to the surface again. This relates to the act of dreaming where we dip into the unconscious realm and return to the surface of consciousness upon awakening.

PENDULUM (*see* **TRAPEZE**)

PENIS (*see* **GENITALIA**)

PERFUME

Perfume, and indeed other smells in dreams, often cast us back into personal history in a way that no image or sound can. From birth, or perhaps before, we associate smell with our parents, homes, and every other experience. What does the perfume evoke in your memory?

PERSEPHONE

Persephone is a goddess who dwells part of the year in the underworld and part of it above ground. She symbolizes the coming of spring, or the approach of winter. Other dream elements will indicate which of these meanings she represents.

PETRIFIED MATERIAL

Petrified objects are old. Medusa and the Gorgon were able to turn people to stone, and Lot's wife met her end as a pillar of salt. Each of these instances has a serious downside, yet petrifaction is part of the process of life, and is therefore natural and proper. A petrified dream image may take on the quality of great age, or it may indicate that you may safely allow the object or person to move out of your life. Petrified bones symbolize a reach into prehistoric developmental processes.

Phallus

Any long object in a dream can be considered to be a phallus. Each object, however, has its own nature as well. In the modern era of greater sexual freedom, most such objects represent themselves, unless they have magical or other meanings. Phallic objects have the qualities of linearity, direction, and sometimes speed. A phallus may occur in dreams when you are focusing your waking attention on sexuality or, paradoxically, when you are denying that part of your emotional being.

Pheasant (*see also* Grouse)

The pheasant symbolizes daylight and daytime hours.

Phoenix

The phoenix is a mythical bird that died in flames and then rose from the ashes. It therefore symbolizes of the ability to resurrect yourself from difficult circumstances. In a dream the phoenix symbolizes transformation and rebirth. It alludes to the successful completion of a difficult process.

Pictures

A picture in a dream is a static representation of something that has life and movement. It may serve to remind you of something you have not seen for a long time, or it may be something you have never seen. The content of the picture tells its own story.

Pig (Boar) (*see also* Hog)

The pig can symbolize the obvious qualities of greed, inconsiderate behavior, and messiness. It can also indicate a deepening of your connection to the earth and the Earth Mother. It also symbolizes the riches of food and other material things. Pigs are very intelligent animals, so the pig may be speaking to your intelligence. The boar is a hostile force, while the pig is gentler.

Pigeon

The pigeon symbolizes the ability to communicate over long distances and could thus indicate telepathic communication or the more ordinary telephone. It also indicates the ability to find your way home either literally, or in the dream processes. It may indicate a desire to go home.

PILGRIM

Voyaging pilgrims and travelers symbolize a spiritual voyage or thought. The pilgrim seeks a center of religious or spiritual belief. The path toward greater knowledge or awareness also implies a return to the creator.

PILLAR

A single pillar symbolizes man and his reach for the heavens. Two pillars indicate the choice between the light and dark paths of the Kabala.

PINE TREE

Pine trees symbolize immortality, and pine cones symbolize life and fertility.

PINK

Sometimes associated with the planet Venus and the sign Libra, pink is the color of babies who are in a state of purity. Pink also reflects unconditional love.

PISCES

The twelfth sign of the zodiac symbolizes the dissolution of forms into the sea of unconsciousness. Vishnu, a Hindu god, emerged from the ocean in the form of a fish. The pair of fish in the sign of the zodiac reflect the dual processes of involution and evolution. Although this sign is often associated with self-denial, it also relates to the quality of empathy and the capacity for compassionate action.

PLAIT (*see* BRAIDS)

PLANETS

The planets in their orbits symbolize the regulated functions of life, as well as the cyclical nature of all human experience.

PLANTS

The general size and health of any plants in your dream are important, as they reflect your own sense of health. Exotic plants symbolize ideas or feelings that are outside your usual range. Cultivated areas reflect an orderly mind, while jungles or weeds suggest a wild element in your thinking and perhaps a toughness that you have or seek.

PLEIADES (SEVEN SISTERS)

The Seven Sisters recall the mystical meaning of the number itself, and also the central role of the planets and stars in our metaphysical and metaphorical lives. This constellation is the stated source of much of the channeled material currently being published.

PLOW

The plow symbolizes humanity's values achieved through crop cultivation—stability, security, and the union of male and female in lasting relationships.

POLE

The pole is the mystic center in many traditions, from the maypole at the center of the dance to the magnetic poles of the earth that define the planet's direction of movement. The pole is the unmoving center of a spinning object, and thus denotes both movement and stillness. In a dream a pole can be seen as defining both direction and center for you.

POMEGRANATE

The pomegranate is a powerful symbol of the feminine, incorporating, as it does, the redness of blood, the multiplicity of seeds, and the capacity for ripening.

POOP (*see* EXCREMENT)

POPLAR

A tall, fast-growing tree, the poplar symbolizes life.

PORCUPINE (HEDGEHOG)

As with many animals, the porcupine shows us two sides of its nature. The dream porcupine may indicate that you need to protect yourself, and may show you how. The porcupine suggests a prickly nature that demands trust and permits no lapses. Yet even the porcupine has its tender side, and can be approached with honesty and openness. The porcupine symbolizes a good-natured person, but the vulnerable side may be well hidden. Its relative, the hedgehog, can be a fun pet, but only if you treat it with respect and earn its trust.

PORPOISE (*see also* DOLPHIN)

A playful aquatic mammal, the porpoise symbolizes the playful attitude you can bring to communicating with the unconscious side of your psyche. The capacity for communication depends on the effective use of words, sounds, and body language.

POTION

Most potions are designed to attract or keep a lover. Generally there is misfortune attached to it, as it goes against the normal rhythm of things. What is the purpose of the potion in your dream?

POWER

While power itself is hard to depict, its agents are frequent dream figures. From lightning to strong men to the immutable force of a flood, we recognize power in the people and things around us. When a dream image conveys this sense of power, it demands that you focus on it and understand its message. If you sit and meditate on the image for a few moments, you may discover another quality underlying the obvious feeling of power.

POWERS (*see* ANGELS)

PRAYING MANTIS

The mantis is said to be praying because of the way it holds its front legs. Yet the mantis employs a vicious tearing process when attacking. The mantis therefore symbolizes both a meditative posture and a pose of attack you may occasionally need to employ. The power of the mantis comes from its ability to remain utterly still. When it appears you may want to meditate to calm your mind. Then new insights may arise and intuition may develop. The kung fu Mantis Form employs linear strikes that are relentless and unswerving. A mantis in your dream may indicate that you need to stick to one thing at a time and do that thing well.

PRIEST (see HIEROPHANT)

PRIESTESS (see HIGH PRIESTESS)

PRIME MATTER (PRIMA MATERIA)

First matter (*prima materia*) is the initial "stuff" we each begin with. Throughout life we work to refine first matter—cleanse and purify it—until it becomes the brilliant diamond of the pure soul. The base matter is associated with the unconscious, while the refined stone is associated with spiritual wisdom.

PRINCE

The prince in fairy tales is the person who goes on a quest, finds the fair maiden, rescues her, and lives happily ever after. He is also the person who must wrestle with demons (basically of his own making) before he can reach his intended goal. His intuition is his finest tool.

PRINCIPALITIES (see ANGELS)

PROCESSION

The procession shares much symbolism with the pilgrimage. There is an implied recession to follow, and the direction of the march is fortified by the number of participants. The symbolism incorporates order and control with power found in numbers.

PROMETHEUS

Prometheus stole fire from the gods and gave it to humanity. The price was eternal pain and suffering for him, but Hercules rescued him from his torment. The fire element symbolizes the value of intuition in your dream. Prometheus' punishment was to have his liver eaten each day by an eagle (or vulture). Liver is the organ associated with anger in many holistic systems, and so is fire. Prometheus gave fire as a gift and paid with his own liver. Consider the roles of fire, anger and giving in the context of your dream.

PROMISED LAND
The Promised Land is the spiritual center for Jews and symbolizes your own center.

PUN
A dream pun is given to you by the Trickster, an archetypal figure who lives to trick you into self-awareness. A pun has two or more meanings that are seemingly different, but linked by more than the mere words. Seek the connections within the pun.

PUPPET (*see* DOLL)

PURPLE
Purple is the color of the crown chakra, of royalty, of church vestments during Lent and Advent, and of power and spirituality.

PYRAMID
The pyramid rises from the flat plain and reaches toward heaven. Yet it is massively heavy and denotes the solidity of earth. In the dream it symbolizes the meeting place between earth and sky. The pyramid is the meeting place of intention and understanding one's action. The pyramid's mass may reflect the apparent weight of all past and future karma, and the pinnacle is the goal of purified spirit.

QUADRANGLE
A quadrangle is any four-sided figure. The shape of it, and the amount of distortion (if any), indicate the slant you take on the world.

QUAIL (*see* GROUSE, PHEASANT)

QUEEN (*see also* KING)
The dream queen may be a projection of yourself. The dream may present your best side as a queen if you are a woman, or the best of your unconscious if you are a man. The queen symbolizes power, as she is the unconscious part of your personality. She is somehow unreachable, and therefore even more desirable.

RABBIT (*see* HARE)

RACCOON

The raccoon symbolizes a capacity for clever manipulation of one's surroundings. It also has a mask and suggests that you can disguise your own thoughts and feelings, or that someone around you is doing so. The strongest symbolism of the raccoon is curiosity—the raccoon, like you, is interested in just about everything.

RADIANCE

A person or object with radiant light around it indicates numinosity or an attractive magnetic quality. The light may be an aura that you could potentially see when awake, although you may not be aware of it. Colors of the aura indicate the general health and emotional currents surrounding the person or object. Halos are one example of radiant light.

RAGS (TATTERS)

Torn clothing indicates an injury done to the person wearing them. The injury can be physical, but often it is emotional or spiritual in nature. The figure in tatters is seen by your dream mind as damaged in some way. When you think about the dream, you may be able to recall the figure into consciousness and actively imagine turning the rags into whole garments, thereby healing the wounds. If the person is known to you, such meditations can be of value to him or her.

RAIN (*see also* DELUGE, OCEAN, RAINBOW, REEFS, RIVER, WATER, WAVE, WETNESS)

Rain uses its element, water, to link air and earth. It symbolizes the interaction between the practical, sensual world and the realm of objective thought. Feelings enliven this pair and make the results come alive. In your dream rain brings the possibility of resolution to a question or problem you are working on because it links objectivity to practical action.

RAINBOW (*see also* DELUGE, OCEAN, RAIN, REEFS, RIVER, WATER, WAVE, WETNESS)

The rainbow symbolizes hope. In a dream it also indicates good fortune to come. It indicates a link between your human and spiritual awareness. If the conditions are right, as light through a waterfall or sprinkler, you can see the rainbow as a complete circle. But whether or not you see the full rainbow, you are the center of this symbol of wholeness, and thus are the focus of the rainbow's energy.

RATS

Often associated with disease, infirmity, or death, the rat is also curious and exploratory. In Chinese astrology, the rat is used to designate the first year of a cycle, and rat people are thought to be shrewd, success-driven, and somewhat restless. The rat is a social animal that stores food and is very adaptable. In a dream the rat most likely symbolizes a restlessness of emotion or spirit—a desire to work toward beneficial change.

RATTLESNAKE

The rattlesnake is integral to Central American cultures. The Mayan new year started at the time the rattlesnake shed its old skin and revealed a new one. Thus the rattlesnake is associated with time and the Mayan calendar. The many uses of rattlesnake patterns in Mayan art reflect the connection of the serpent to divine creativity, and remind you in the dream of your creative processes. The diamond pattern on the snake's skin was used to define human physical proportions, patterns in fabric, and structural elements in buildings. In addition, this pattern is closely connected to the Mayan calendar, and the snakes on certain pyramids light up as the sun rises on the spring equinox.

RAVEN

Ravens have long symbolized magic. A raven in a dream indicates that magical change is in the air. The raven may speak of the great mysteries of life and provide the energy needed to delve into the unknown realms of consciousness. The raven is an omen and a messenger. Pay attention to the raven's seemingly ordinary actions in the dream, as they may be profoundly important. You may want to meditate in order to create a space for the raven's message. Otherwise it is easy to ignore the ordinary that cloaks a brilliant connection to the collective intelligence.

RAVINE (see CANYON)

REBIRTH (REBORN)

Rebirth is a powerful archetype. We often find it associated with religious conversion because of its power. Yet we are reborn each day when we awake, and each new idea we encounter sparks another birth within us. If the feeling of being reborn appears in your dream, it symbolizes the power of the dream itself to change your life, and therefore suggests that you give the dream your attention.

RED

In general red reflects the emotions. In the Buddhist system, red reflects discriminating awareness. Passion is associated with this color, as well as blood, the life-force. Red is the color of church vestments for Pentacost or Whitsunday and the color of the root chakra. Typical emotions indicated by red are anger, even rage, and sexual desire.

RED SEA

The Red Sea, or an ocean of red, indicates that blood has been spilled. A sacrifice has been made, just as the Hebrews experienced when leaving Egypt to find the Promised Land.

REEFS (*see also* DELUGE, OCEAN, RAIN, RAINBOW, RIVER, WATER, WAVE, WETNESS)

Just as a reef limits the tidal flow of water along a shore, the dream reef presents an obstacle to the flooding of unconscious material into the mind. In this sense the reef suggests it is barring information that is trying to emerge into consciousness and suggests you need to be cautious with that material.

REINS

Reins indicate potential control over the instinctual realm.

RELIEF

When the feeling of relief arises in a dream, its intensity reflects the level of reality of the dream experience.

RETURN

A return represents the ending of a cycle, and thus a little death of a period of life. The return also indicates the potential for a new beginning, based on the experience gained during the previous cycles.

RHINOCEROS

Thought to possess an aphrodisiac power in its horn, the rhinoceros is a powerful animal symbolic of instinctual impulses. In a dream the rhino symbolizes the sense of smell, as the rhino's horn is on its nose. The sense of smell is perhaps the earliest of the senses to develop in animals. The smell of a flower or an old book can evoke the oldest memories. The rhinoceros may be symbolizing a need, a desire, or the action of reaching back into your memory to reclaim something of importance.

RIBBONS

Ribbons indicate victory and high placement. Even hair ribbons share this quality. Braided ribbons indicate the weaving together perhaps of other dream images into a unified reality.

RING

The ring shares the symbolism of the circle without beginning or end. Rings are used to symbolize love shared between individuals, and also indicate the cyclical nature of life.

RITE (CEREMONY)

Any ceremony partakes in the qualities of ritual, and as such is both socially satisfying and spiritually valuable. A rite brings together forces and patterns of energy and applies them to the purpose of the event.

RIVER (*see also* **DELUGE, OCEAN, RAIN, RAINBOW, REEFS, WATER, WAVE, WETNESS**)

Flowing water can symbolize a nurturing quality, the emotion of raging anger in a flood, and the flow of time. It symbolizes irreversible processes.

ROADRUNNER

Roadrunner cartoons portray a wily bird who outwits a coyote again and again. A roadrunner can run very fast, and generally does not fly, although it retains a rudimentary ability to do so. This bird symbolizes mental agility—the ability to run after one idea, change directions, or double back. You are familiar with the tendency of your thoughts to almost run away with you; yet the capacity for swift thought is a sign of intellectual strength. The roadrunner is able to stop on a dime to consider its next action, and it symbolizes this ability within you.

ROBIN

One of the first signs of spring, the robin heralds a new season of growth and plenty. In a dream it symbolizes the capacity to nurture and expand, as well as symbolizing independence.

ROCK (STONE)

Rock represents the earth element and therefore symbolizes stability and permanence.

ROOF

The roof of a building provides protection from the sun and the weather. A steep roof symbolizes the ability to shed ideas or feelings that are not useful. A flat roof symbolizes the capacity to soak up the energy of mental and spiritual life.

ROOM

An individual room symbolizes individuality itself. The nature of the room and its furnishings may reveal something about your own sense of self—your private thoughts. The furnishings may have literal or metaphorical meaning.

ROOSTER (*see* **COCK**)

ROPE (CORD, STRING)

Rope, cord, and string share connecting and binding symbolism. Binding suggests limitation and restriction of movement, while connecting suggests flow, either between the connected objects, or because one object is used to move the other, as in one vehicle towing another. In a dream a rope that is simply there, not tying anything, still retains this symbolism.

ROSE (*see* **LOTUS**)

ROTATION
Rotation marks the boundary of a circle, and thus has a magical quality of protection and power.

ROUND TABLE
The Round Table gathered Arthur and his knights together in the spirit of equality to pursue a shared vision. Any round table or object implies the centering of body, mind, and spirit.

RUDDER
A dream rudder symbolizes the capacity to steer. It tells you that you can plot a course through the dream, and therefore through your waking challenges.

RUINS
Because buildings so often symbolize the body, ruins symbolize the feeling of physical injury. They also remind you of ancient ideas or feelings that may or may not deal with injury, but that are time-worn. If the ruins are repaired in this or other dreams or in active imagination, it suggests that while the ideas seem outdated, they may be useful in the present.

S

SACRIFICE
A sacrifice is the giving up of one thing to gain another of equal or greater value. In a dream it may mean that you are faced with a choice between two or more things that presently have equal value. The dream may be offering insight into which choice to make.

SAGITTARIUS
The ninth sign of the zodiac reflects its dual nature in the horse-man figure. The sign has its roots in instinct yet reflects human intellect. The arrow points to the spiritual level to indicate a third component of this sign.

SAILS
Sails fill with wind and therefore symbolize of the air element, or logical thought put into action.

SALAMANDER

This animal is believed to be able to survive in fire, and symbolizes your ability to survive the heat of embarrassment, shame, or other misfortunes. It also symbolizes the purifying capacity of fire.

SALMON (TROUT)

The salmon is an indication that determination is part of your dream and waking life. The salmon overcomes huge odds to fight its way upstream to spawn, and you too can overcome odds to achieve success. Both trout and salmon indicate that you are comfortable with your emotions and strong enough to manage them well.

SANDWICH

Sandwiches reflect the ability to contain one thing or idea within another. They also indicate the ability to do two things at once. Consider the meaning of both the bread (the container) and the filling (the part that needs to be contained in order to make it useful).

SARCOPHAGUS (*see* **TOMB**)

SATURN

Saturn most frequently symbolizes the passage of time. Just as Cronos devoured each if his offspring as they were born, time consumes all physical things. Saturn therefore symbolizes limitation. Astrologically Saturn rules the skin, teeth, and bones, and therefore symbolizes the principle of structure.

SCALES

Any symmetrical figure suggests balance. Scales indicate a balanced approach to materials within a dream. The scales of justice are one example of balancing two polarities. On the higher spiritual level, any action, good or bad, brings its results in the form of immediate reaction or karma, which may work out in the future. The scales we find on fish offer layered protection along with flexibility.

SCARAB

Sacred to the Egyptians, this beetle can be found represented in jewelry and art. It is a fetish—a kind of charm that symbolizes metamorphosis, the trait shared by all insects. The scarab is associated with the expected resurrection of Egyptian royalty. In a dream the scarab symbolizes your ability to survive and to change.

SCARS

Scars or blemishes in a dream symbolize areas where the dream figure has suffered, or is in some way deficient. It is important to consider these two possibilities carefully, as they are remarkably different in meaning.

Scepter (*see also* **Wand**)

The scepter or wand holds, at least symbolically, the power of the individual owner. The configuration of the dream wand reflects its purpose and power. Size is not a good indication of relative power in this kind of tool. Rather, the wand or scepter indicates that its bearer has innate power.

Scissors

Scissors have two parts that meet and work together. This tool symbolizes beginnings and endings, as it severs the cord at birth and the thread of life at death.

Scorpio

The eighth sign of the zodiac refers to death, but also to regeneration and rebirth. The sign is depicted as the scorpion, the eagle, or the phoenix.

Scorpion

This desert animal is said to sting itself to death when cornered, and has a deadly reputation because of its poisonous quality. It is associated with Scorpio, the eighth sign of the zodiac, and symbolizes death and rebirth. In your dream the scorpion may evoke a feeling of fear. This feeling is a communication from the unconscious, and can indicate an imbalance between your waking life and your unconscious psyche. The scorpio also symbolizes the protective capacity you have built into your mental processes.

Screw (*see* **Bolt**)

Scythe

The tool of Saturn, the scythe symbolizes the passage of time.

Sea (*see* **Deluge, Ocean, Rain, Rainbow, Reefs, River, Wave, Wetness**)

Sea Dragon (*see* **Leviathan**)

Sea Horse

The sea horse symbolizes the power of the ocean, and therefore the unconscious part of your psyche. In a dream a sea horse may indicate unconscious movement or a change in your outlook.

Seagull (*see* **Gull**)

Seal

The seal's capacity to play symbolizes your dream ability to play with symbols, ideas, and feelings, rearranging them until they come into a sensible pattern that renews your being. We achieve new balance and clarity by playing with ideas and not allowing them to stagnate. The seal may also symbolize the capacity to use different thoughts and feelings in our lives.

Seal of Solomon (*see* Star of David)

Seasons
The passage of the seasons symbolizes the stages of life, from birth and youth to old age and death.

Secret
Secrets carry power. A dream secret is the revealing of something that has been hidden, but now needs to emerge into consciousness. Such a secret offers you its power.

Seed
Seeds symbolize latent power. The acorn may sprout into the oak. The mustard seed is a symbol of hope. The seed also symbolizes one's spiritual center.

Seeing Eye Dog
Completely loyal and attentive to the task at hand, the Seeing Eye dog symbolizes a part of yourself that cannot be deterred from its purpose. The daimon is that part—the inner voice that drives you to fulfill your deepest dreams and desires, and which redirects you to the proper path when you have strayed.

Sephiroth
There are ten Sephirah, or emanations of god, in Kabala. The ten Sephirah are Crown, Wisdom, Understanding, Mercy, Severity, Beauty, Victory, Splendor, Foundation, and Kingdom. The pathways among these serve as lessons for the initiate.

Self
When you become aware of the self in your dream, it symbolizes a center of your being that you may not ordinarily experience in waking life. The self is not all of you, or even all "you." It symbolizes wholeness, but is not wholeness. The self in your dream brings a potent message about your current direction and asks for recognition and consideration.

Seraphim (*see* Angels)

Serpent (Snake) (*see also* Ouroboros)
Snakes symbolize the potent force of spirit. Egyptian priests believed the snake symbolized their connection with the gods. Because it sheds its skin in order to grow, the snake is a powerful symbol of transmutation. In a dream it may be showing you that you have been or are about to be transformed. In spite of the biblical serpent who convinced Eve to eat the apple that caused the downfall of mankind, the serpent is a powerful creative force when it appears in your dreams.

SEVEN

Seven is a number of harmony. It is the number of notes in the musical scale, the colors of the rainbow, the directions (when you include above, below, and the center), and the days of the week. When seven appears in a dream, consider how your life is resonating with this number. In metaphysics the seventh heaven is where you go when you have completed all earthly tasks.

SEVEN SISTERS (*see* PLEIADES)

SEX

The act of copulation symbolizes the union of opposites. Psychologically it refers to the union of the conscious and unconscious elements of the mind. It also refers to the union of the masculine and feminine aspects within the individual personality. Finally it symbolizes the alchemical process of purification and of union. Sexual differences are among the most profound polarities we experience in everything. They indicate the relationship between strength and weakness, black and white, light and dark, and so on. They also indicate spiritual principles of movement, as between heaven and earth, or death and rebirth.

Psychic energy can be expressed in many ways besides sexual libido, but sex is certainly one very powerful expression. Therefore it is helpful not to dismiss your sexual feelings too soon when you awake from such a dream. How do you feel about the erotic images in your dream? Is there a sense of satisfaction in this dream?

In Jungian psychology, the act of sex is viewed as a metaphor for the inner union of masculine and feminine. Whether you are male or female, the union of opposites portrayed in the act of intercourse may be a visual representation of your own adult developmental process in which you are coming to terms with the conscious and less conscious facets of your sexuality. Are you aware of changes in how you relate to your inner life?

Sexual activity in a dream may relate to other creative activities, including the power to heal and the power to insure the earth's fertility. Sexual images may be graphic representations of creative work that has yet to emerge fully from the mental process into physical manifestation. Your dream may be a firm symbolic confirmation that your creative activities are moving in a good direction.

SEXUAL IMAGES (*see* EROTICISM)

SHADOW

Shadows in dreams symbolize the hidden, perhaps less-acceptable side of any dream object. When Peter Pan lost his shadow, this was viewed as a crisis because the inner, hidden part of the psyche is necessary to life and to normal function. Without it there would be no dreams, and possibly no inspiration. The Shadow is a figure unique to you that incorporates the part of your mind that has been hidden or repressed, usually because in some way it is unacceptable to the conscious mind. It includes both destructive and constructive aspects, all of which conflict with your present conscious sense of yourself. The Shadow is a source of conflict, but once recognized and accepted, it is a source of rich material for self-development.

Sharp (*see* Axes, Knife, Sword)

Sheaf

A sheaf of grain symbolizes civilization. Thus it incorporates both the limitation of social requirements with the freedom allowed by the accumulation of food. It symbolizes integration within the mind and spirit, and therefore strength.

Shell

Shells symbolize the purifying and sustaining qualities of water. They also symbolize the security and protection of the home.

Shepherd

The shepherd symbolizes leadership and protection. In a dream this figure may also symbolically represent the organizing function of the mind.

Shield

The shield is an implement of protection: in battle against the enemy, in bad weather against the elements. In a dream the shield may symbolize emotional or spiritual protection.

Ship

A ship symbolizes movement. It carries us across water and protects us from drowning. Psychologically the ship or boat allows us to touch the unconscious without falling into it too deeply.

Shirt (Blouse, Tunic) (*see also* Clothes)

A blouse or shirt, like any garment, is worn first to protect the body (from cold, rain, the sun, etc.) and second to suit social requirements of dress. The style of the garment may suggest a trip back in history to another time. A departure from the normal style of clothing may indicate that you are entertaining, in your unconscious life, the possibility of becoming someone different—taking a different job, moving to a different climate, and so on.

Shoes

Shoes symbolize understanding. They also symbolize the freedom of movement that they provide, and thus indicate a sense of liberty (which understanding often provides).

SIEVE (*see* COMB)

SIGMA

The eighteenth letter of the Greek alphabet symbolizes the spiral path of spiritual development. It also symbolizes the flow of water downhill, and therefore the progression of events in a predictable direction. It also reflects the changing phases of the moon, and therefore suggests change when it appears in a dream.

SIGN

Any dream image can be a sign that you evaluate for yourself. Signs are the outward indication of an inner emotional or spiritual reality. A road sign indicates a hidden danger, or points to a distant place that cannot yet be seen. Generally signs intend to be helpful, providing information you may not otherwise have been aware of.

SILVER

Associated with the moon and night, silver represents a condition of being easy to work with. In a dream it may represent a state of mind that allows change to take place. Thus it indicates adaptability, just as the moon is a symbol of change. It may be present when the unconscious offers you messages.

SIREN (MERMAID) (*see also* LORELEI)

The siren symbolizes temptation. In a dream the siren may stand in for the temptation, or may appear with it. The siren is generally thought to be destructive, but it is this kind of attraction that makes us aware of creative potential and drives us to succeed in life.

SIX

Six is a balanced number and symbolizes the equilibrium of the mind when it is working harmoniously, or harmonious relationships between or among people. The Star of David has six points and includes two triangles, one pointing up toward heaven and one pointing down toward earth. It symbolizes the union of heaven and earth, or of god and goddess, or man and woman.

SKELETON (*see also* BONE)

Skeletons represent death. However, the skeleton is also the part of the body that allows effective movement and that provides structure for the softer organs. Therefore the skeleton symbolizes life structure.

SKIN

Skin symbolizes rebirth. The skin renews itself continually. The snake sheds its skin as it grows. The skin also symbolizes the container. Skins can be used to carry water, food, and other paraphernalia. Removing the skin or hide of something symbolizes of reaching deeper into the hidden meaning of things.

SKULL

Skulls are used in both Western and Eastern cultures to symbolize mortality. The skull is the physical remains after the spirit has left and the flesh has dissolved. The skull also is the symbolic container of thought, and therefore intelligence.

SKUNK

The skunk in your dreams symbolizes reputation—and it is up to you to determine whether yours "smells" or not. You can engender respect in others if you mean what you say and say what you mean. The skunk moves about, minds its own business, and only sprays when it is challenged. The skunk tells you to learn the best way to assert yourself without causing others to "spray" you. Prepare to be noticed by others if the skunk appears in your life.

SKYSCRAPER

The skyscraper symbolizes the height of success that human beings can reach. It also symbolizes the aspiration to reach for higher spiritual awareness. Tall buildings parallel towers in spiritual symbolism.

SLEEPING BEAUTY

Sleeping Beauty symbolizes the masculine anima dormant in the unconscious. She symbolizes passive potential, not yet activated in consciousness.

SLUG

Slimy and low, the slug seemingly has little to redeem in a dream. However, it is thought to represent the male aspect of the creative process. It does have the quality of steady, persistent movement. In a dream it may symbolize the part of your being that seems to move painfully slowly toward a goal. The point, however, is that there is movement.

SMOKE

Smoke incorporates the fire and air elements into visible form, yet the form is utterly elusive. Smoke has the magical capacity in rituals to ward off negative energies. Being carried by smoke allows you to astral travel or spread your consciousness over wide areas.

SNAIL

A slow creature, the snail symbolizes steady effort toward a goal. The snail's shell has a spiral form that expresses a balanced geometry. Because the spiral pattern is sacred in religion and geometry, the snail has a spiritually elevating attribute. In a dream it may indicate that a "snail's pace" is just fine for the present.

SNAKE (*see* OUROBOROS, SERPENT)

SNARE (*see* ENTANGLEMENT, NET, SPIDER, SPIDER WOMAN, SPINNING, WEAVING)

SOLUTION (*see* WETNESS)

SOPHIA (GUIDE)

Sophia, the gnostic Great Mother, is one manifestation of the anima as a spiritual guide. In Hebrew tradition she is the Shekinah, or light at the center of creation. A feminine guide in a dream provides a path or perspective that has been unavailable in your waking life. A masculine guide may suggest a precise direction, while a feminine guide suggests general themes and circular or spiral directions.

SORCERER

The sorcerer symbolizes the Terrible Father, a generally evil figure. At the same time he symbolizes the power inherent in all things—a power you must grasp firmly and understand in order to use effectively.

SOUND

Sound is the oldest thing we know. Music was the source of all creation in Hindu beliefs, while the Word was what God used to create the world in Jewish and Christian traditions. Many people have utterly silent dreams. Others regularly experience auditory phenomena in dreams. The quality of the sound is important to consider, as well as the musical or literal content.

SOUTH

South is the direction of conscious thought, and of self-awareness. Travelling there in a dream means you are seeking to understand yourself better.

SPACE (VOID) (*see also* ABYSS, EMPTINESS, MACROCOSM, NOTHINGNESS)

Space has been called the final frontier because we have explored almost every inch of the planet earth. Images from space have redefined how we view our own planet. Space and space travel symbolize the pioneering spirit in us. While you may not aspire to actually travel in space, the dream offers insight into your inner pioneering impulse.

SPARK

The spark symbolizes the inner creative process. It also symbolizes the soul.

SPARROW

The sparrow symbolizes inner dignity and the nobility of the small.

Sparrow Hawk (Falcon) (*see also* Hawk)

Symbolic of the sun for the ancient Egyptians, the sparrow hawk symbolizes agility of movement and mind.

Sphinx

The sphinx is one of the great mysteries of the ancient world, and in a dream it signals that you are close to understanding a mystery. We still don't understand how the sphinx was built and how it has survived for so many centuries. In a dream the sphinx may symbolize the capacity for reincarnation, and certainly the mysterious factors in our daily lives. It may be appearing to suggest silence as a path of action as well.

Spider (Snare, Web)
(*see also* Entanglement, Net, Spider Woman, Spinning, Weaving)

Spiders have played a role in mythology around the world. The Spider Woman provides the creative impulse to weave for American Indians, and was associated with weaving for the ancient Greeks as well. The spider has several symbolic meanings: First, it has the power to create, indicated by its web. Second, it is aggressive in the treatment of its prey. Third, the pattern of the web is reminiscent of the spiral of life, a profound symbol of progressive development. Hindus thought the spider wove the web of *maya,* or illusion. The thread of life and death symbolizes the pattern of rebirth.

Spider Woman (Snare, Web)
(*see also* Entanglement, Net, Spider, Spinning, Weaving)

In Pueblo Indian tradition, the Spider Woman was also called Thinking Woman. In primordial times, she was said to have sat alone, spinning in the four directions to create the sun, moon, and then people. Navajo weavers always incorporate a slight flaw in their carpets, as they recognize the inspiration of the Spider Woman and do not wish to offend her by weaving a perfect rug. Mythology around the world includes one or more women who weave birth, life, and death into their fabrics. The Spider Woman is a great source of wisdom concerning your life.

Spindle (Bobbin)

The spindle and bobbin symbolize life and its length. They also refer to the cyclical nature of life, including the planets and the moon. The spiral wrapping of the thread indicates a psychological spiral into the self, or the reversal of direction.

Spinning (Snare, Web)
(*see also* Entanglement, Net, Spider, Spider Woman, Weaving)

Spinning, webs, weaving, and fabric are all symbols of the unfolding of life.

SPIRAL

The spiral embodies the mystical quality of life and evolution. It suggests movement that, while basically going around a central core, moves in an upward or downward direction. DNA spirals are a fundamental component of physical life. The dream spiral symbolizes cosmic forces that are in motion in the dream. The developmental process involves a spiral path around the center of your being by which you come to understand yourself more fully. Kundalini energy spirals up the spine, moving spiritual energies throughout the body. The static spiral of a snail shell is a natural logarithm caused by physical growth. The expanding spiral of galaxies shows the potential scope of unlimited spirit. The inward spiral of a whirlpool suggests movement into the unconscious as a result of concentrated energy.

SPRING

Spring is the season in which life, the trees and the animals, burst forth from the earth. It symbolizes the potential resurrection of the spirit, and appears in dreams to indicate that the growth cycle has begun. In a spring setting, dream figures are often seen as helpers.

SPUR

Spurs symbolize action.

SQUARE (GRAPHICS)

The square can be found in nature (e.g., in salt crystals). It is the basic element of the framework for building construction: the horizontal floor piece, the perpendicular pieces for the walls, the horizontal piece for the ceiling. While pyramids are triangular in overall form, they are composed of blocks of stone that have perpendicular faces. The term *foursquare* describes solid construction that can be expected to last, and also solid precepts that can withstand the test of time.

SQUIRREL

An industrious creature, the squirrel saves up stores stores of food to avoid starving in winter.

STAFF

The staff has two symbolic meanings: (1) an implement for support, as a walking staff, and (2) a weapon for punishment or defense.

STAG

The antlers of the stag remind us of the branches of a tree, and in some cultures they symbolize the Tree of Life. The ability to regenerate antlers symbolizes the cycle of life through rebirth. The stag has mystical gifts—grace and agility—and thus may indicate in your dream the condition of rising to greater heights of mind. It certainly indicates of nobility of mind and spirit, and is therefore an uplifting symbol.

STAIRS (ELEVATOR, ESCALATOR, LADDER, PATH) (*see also* STEPS)

Stairs and stairways indicate movement between levels of consciousness. The movement downward or upward—spiritually, mentally, physically, and/or emotionally in the unconscious or collective unconscious—is consistent across cultures, although the images vary widely. For example, winding stairways may lead to various basements, subbasements, and so on, or a sloping path may lead into a deep underground cave. The attic of a house may indicate a space where personal thoughts are accessed, or you may see high rocky ground or a platform in a tree. A path may lead into a field or forest, indicating another kind of change in consciousness. Ladders have utilitarian uses, but reflect the same kind of movement or change as stairs and paths. All three—ladders, stairs, and paths—symbolize forward or backward movement.

STAR

Stars symbolize the spirit. They also indicate multiplicity of energies. The five-pointed star symbolizes the five elements in Chinese cosmology. The pentagram is used in magic rituals. The center of the figure is implied, not shown, and it symbolizes the center of being or spirit.

In tarot, the Star is the seventeenth card of the Major Arcana. It reflects the interrelationship among worlds, bringing the celestial down to earth and connecting it to material world. The ultimate symbolism is of spirit connected to matter.

STAR OF DAVID (HEXAGRAM, SEAL OF SOLOMON)

The six-pointed star is actually two triangles overlapping each other. It symbolizes spiritual potential. The triangles symbolize fire and water. Their interaction is that of intuition and judgment.

STARE (*see* GLANCE)

STARFISH

The five arms of the starfish symbolize the five elements in the Chinese alchemical system (water, wood, metal, fire, and earth), and the elements fire, earth, air, water, and ether in the Western alchemical tradition. The starfish also reflects our human form (arms, legs, and head). The five legs reflect the five senses. The form embodies the "golden mean," a proportion that is particularly pleasing to the eye perhaps because it conforms to human physical proportions. In your dream the starfish symbolizes your ability to consider many options in the decision-making process, as well as your ability to try one or more of them in your pursuit of success and fulfillment.

STEED

Any animal that can carry you in a dream symbolizes your ability to use instinctual processes in the pursuit of intellectual or spiritual goals. It may also symbolize the physical body.

STEEL

Steel is the refined and hardened result of processing iron. Beginning with iron's strength, the process results in a flexible yet strong building element. Hardness here may be equated to toughness.

STEPS (ELEVATOR, ESCALATOR, LADDER, PATH) (*see also* STAIRS)

Steps or stairs going up imply ascension into the realm of thought or spirit, while steps going down imply descent into the unconscious. The same can be said of elevators. Thus in a dream you can move between various levels of consciousness simply by using the stairway provided. The number of steps, rungs, or levels measures the degree of ascent or descent from your normal conscious level.

STICK

A stick can be a wand, thereby imbued with magical capabilities. It may also be a stirring or drawing implement. The quality of the stick itself symbolizes the magic or the success of the process. An old stick may suggest well-used methodology.

STONE (*see* ROCK)

STORK

In China and other cultures, the stork is associated with new birth. In Western culture children are told that the stork brought them to their parents. A stork in your dream can mean a new birth—of a child, or of an idea. The stork also engages in an almost ritualistic mating dance, reminding us of the sacred dances humans perform for fertility and other purposes.

STORM

While thunderstorms are often experienced as destructive forces, they also bring life-sustaining rain, and therefore have a creative aspect. A storm of activity can be very productive, such as a brainstorm.

STRANGER

Strangers in dreams are often compelling in whatever they say or do. You notice them more in many cases than you would a familiar figure. They symbolize the potential for change that has not entered conscious awareness.

Stream (*see* **Ford**)

Strength

In tarot, the eleventh card of the Major Arcana shows that physical power is not the essence of strength. Rather, power comes from effective use of energy. Thus strength symbolizes the use of intelligence.

String (*see* **Rope**)

Subterranean Places (*see* **Cave**)

Sulfur

This yellowish element is useful in creating fire and symbolizes a specific stage in the alchemical process. It indicates a developmental stage where intellect and intuition are engaged. In a dream it symbolizes a higher level of reasoning.

Summer

Summer is the season of growth and maturation in nature. It symbolizes the growth of one's knowledge and the expansion of one's range of influence in the world. Dream figures in summer settings are often viewed as companions or equals.

Sun

The sun is the center of the solar system, and symbolizes the spiritual center of being. In tarot, the nineteenth card of the Major Arcana symbolizes spirit, the true source of riches. In many tarot decks the Sun suggests that relationships are one of the most significant ways of gaining spiritual riches.

Sunshade (Umbrella)

The sunshade or umbrella brings together sunlight and protection from its radiation. Such spiritual protection can also be understood as the container for existence.

Superiority

When a waking world relationship between people or things is different in a dream, it may be a simple inversion of forces. For example, if you seem much larger physically than your boss, the dream is offering you the option of seeing yourself as more important, and further suggests that some aspect of your boss's personality is indeed smaller or less desirable than your own. Because superior is not necessarily better, the dream can also be viewed as an opportunity to explore the relationship between the people or objects involved.

SWALLOW (MARTIN)

A harbinger of summer, the swallow is welcomed around the world. In a dream it symbolizes the ability to fly gracefully, and to avoid becoming fettered by ordinary problems. It is a signal to rise above the day-to-day and gain a broader perspective. The swallow is said to be sacred to Venus and Isis.

SWAMP (*see* MARSH)

SWAN

The grace of a swan is something to be admired and emulated. The swan symbolizes both physical and spiritual beauty, and comes to you in dreams when there is an element of purity in your life.

SWASTIKA

This ancient symbol earned a black name when it was used by the Nazi Party, but its roots suggest a far different interpretation: the swastika originally symbolized the movement of the elements and also the power of the sun. This symbol may be associated with the cardinal directions or with ancient deities. The root word for swastika in Hindi is *svasti*, which means "good luck." The clockwise swastika symbolizes solar, masculine energy, while the counterclockwise swastika denotes feminine and lunar energies.

SWORD (SHARP) (*see also* AXES, KNIFE)

The sword symbolizes the ability to protect oneself and to wound others, figuratively or literally. In religious art the sword is used to cut through misunderstanding and to purify. In secular use the sword indicates courage. A broken sword suggests a lack of, or a destroyed, spiritual purity.

τ

TARANTULA

A tarantula is big and ugly and supposedly very poisonous. Actually, its bite is no more poisonous than a bee sting. The tarantula does its work at home and waits for its food to come to it. When spiders appear in your dreams, it may be time to regroup in private to get your creative projects moving.

TAROT (MAJOR ARCANA)

Tarot cards symbolize the ability to see into the future, or to divine events in the present or past. The deck also symbolizes the whole of intellectual and intuitive wisdom. In addition to the Minor Arcana of four suits (swords, rods, coins, and cups) the traditional tarot deck includes a trump suit (or Major Arcana) of twenty-two cards that describe the spiritual path of life.

TATTERS (*see* **RAGS**)

TATTOOS
Tattoos symbolize a physical, and therefore a mystical sacrifice. The pain involved in its creation is thought to imbue the tattoo itself with protective or other powers. A dream tattoo suggests that you may have powers of which you are unaware.

TAURUS
The second sign of the zodiac is associated with strength and power and the ability to find and maintain comfort. This ability is rooted in the instinctual world. This symbol in a dream may also relate to the throat or ears in some way.

TEETH
Teeth and their condition in a dream symbolize power or inhibited power in the waking world. There is also a sexual connotation according to some interpretations. Clenched teeth may indicate angry emotions, even if there is no other indication of anger in the dream. Teeth falling out can indicate a dental problem, or may indicate fear of losing power.

TELEKINESIS (*see* **EXTRAORDINARY ABILITIES**)

TELEPATHY (*see* **EXTRAORDINARY ABILITIES**)

TEMPERANCE
In tarot, the fourteenth card of the Major Arcana symbolizes the potential for transformation, universal life, and the power found in circulating energy systems.

TEMPLE
The temple is the forehead on the physical body and a point projected above the head that dissects the heavens and contacts the higher spiritual spheres. The temple as a sacred building has similar symbolism in that it is the center of a spiritual or ritual practice.

TEN
Ten indicates a spiritual completion that returns to the number one, or unity. Multiples of ten are more powerful expressions of the base number. Ten is the sum of one, two, three, and four, and is therefore considered a powerful combination of divine energies.

TENT

The tent provides protection from the weather. It symbolizes the protection of spirit that surrounds your individual being. Tents, no matter what they look like, are also reminiscent of the desert and its symbolism.

TEXTURE

Textures, by their appearance and feel, symbolize emotions or evoke memories. Smooth textures suggest aloofness or distance, and therefore coolness, while rough, porous textures suggest warmth and closeness.

THEATER

A dream theater provides a symbolic stage on which dream actors move. Viewing a movie in a dream reflects dissociation from the content of the dream movie, a psychological defense that allows you to observe something without becoming emotionally involved.

THICKET (*see* BRAMBLE)

THIGH

Because the thigh has very large, strong muscles, it symbolizes psychic strength.

THIRST

Thirst in a dream symbolizes an appetite for information that the dream may attempt to provide. Drinking is recommended. If you did not drink anything in the dream, you may want to imagine yourself back in the dream so that you can do so.

THORN

Thorns offer symbolic protection from harm, and imply the value of that which they protect. You may want to think about self-protection when thorns appear in your dreams.

THREAD

Thread symbolizes a connection between realms—physical, social, or spiritual.

THREE

Three is an active number. It is a synthesis of one and two. The three-sided figure is stable—it is difficult to smash or manipulate. The number three may represent a problem-solving situation in which you need to discern three choices in order to make an effective decision.

THRESHOLD

A threshold symbolizes a transition. When you cross a threshold in a dream, you are moving from one stage of experience into another. It symbolizes both the difference and separation of two experiences, and the meaningful connection between them.

THRONE

The throne both exalts and connects the monarch to the physical plane, and thus to the ordinary. Thus if your dream includes a throne, it may serve to elevate you or connect you with royal ideas and people in the dream.

THRONES (*see* ANGELS)

THULE

Thule is a mythic realm. The root word is found in languages around the world. It symbolizes salvation, a place above the realm of physical forms.

THUNDERBIRD

The thunderbird is a mythical bird with many features of the eagle. It is said to control lightning and thunder. If it appears in a dream, it symbolizes the voice of the Great Spirit, and you will want to consider the message carefully.

THUNDERBOLT

The thunderbolt, or lightning, is a dynamic force of nature and symbolizes a comparable psychic force. It symbolizes illumination.

TIE (*see* BOW)

TIGER

Massive muscles ripple as the tiger walks and thrusts its huge paws forward. Fiercely maternal, the females raise the young and teach them to hunt. In Chinese astrology the tiger person is passionate, powerful, and sexual. Tigers may be unpredictable. A tiger in your dreams symbolizes a powerful new direction opening up in your life.

TIME TRAVEL (*see* EXTRAORDINARY ABILITIES)

TIN

This metal is associated with the planet Jupiter. Tin is malleable, yet it holds its shape well. Thus it symbolizes all that is expansive in the spiritual realm. It is used to plate other metals that would otherwise badly tarnish. A tin is a sealed container that preserves its contents. The container may actually be made of aluminum or other elements. Such a container symbolizes the part of the personality that protects the self, and may suggest either the need for protection, or the need to open the sealed container so the contents may be used.

TITANS (*see also* GIANT)

Titans and giants symbolize the wild, untamable portion of the psyche. They often are found in caves, symbolizing the unconscious mind.

TOMB (SARCOPHAGUS)

A tomb symbolizes the body as matter which is dead in itself and must be inspired by spirit to have life. In a dream a tomb can symbolize the quiet place you go to to meditate.

TORCH

The torch is a symbol associated with the sun. It is an emblem of the truth.

TORNADO (see BREEZE, HURRICANE, WIND)

TORTOISE (see TURTLE)

TOWER

The tower symbolizes rising above an ordinary social life, and indicates the desire to ascend to a higher level of experience. In tarot, the sixteenth card of the Major Arcana depicts the destructive force of nature that results from human arrogance. The Tower in a dream suggests that you may be in the midst of a material or psychological setback that will reveal the true nature of your mission in life. It indicates that dependence on the material world is removed and that your spiritual being exists outside of your material situation.

TOYS

Toys represent the temptation to avoid or escape tasks that are not seen as fun. In a dream they may remind you of a time when you had fewer responsibilities, or they may suggest that you need to devote some of your time to play, in order to allow your mind, body, and spirit to regenerate.

TRANSFORMATION (see METAMORPHOSIS)

TRANSMUTATION (see METAMORPHOSIS)

TRAPEZE (PENDULUM)

The trapeze shares the motion of the pendulum. The pendulum in motion produces a regular movement, and it is the regularity that allows circus performers to swing from one to the other so gracefully. Note that the pendulum is still when it is in its most horizontal position, and is moving the fastest when it reaches the vertical position. This reflects the martial arts teaching that a body in motion can respond more quickly than one at rest.

TRAVEL (see JOURNEY)

TREASURE

Treasure in a dream indicates the fruit of your work. This can be psychic effort or on-the-job performance. It represents the transmutation of your energy into something tangible and valuable. In a dream it suggests that you are nearing a goal in your waking life.

TREE

The tree links the three worlds of the unconscious, the material, and the spiritual. A single tree represents a center—of the world or of your personality. It reminds us of the Tree of Life. The tree suggests the duality of conscious life (trunk and branches) supported by the unconscious (root system).

TRIANGLE

In geometry three points describe the circumference of a circle. This means that any triangle represents the entire circle, and thus symbolizes a path without beginning or end. So regardless of the shape of the triangle in your dream, it can be seen as a symbol of continuous energy flow. In alchemy a triangle pointing up represents fire, while one pointing down represents water.

TRICKSTER (*see also* MAGICIAN)

The Trickster is a dream element that arrives to change your perspective. This archetype can take any form. Examples include the clown that is allowed to say or do whatever he wants, or the speaker who uses words that have dual or ambiguous meanings. This kind of dream message is masked so that you will accept it in the dream. When you consciously evaluate it, you may identify the message's dual meaning.

TRIDENT

Neptune and Satan both have a trident as a symbol of their power. Both also reside in the underworld: Neptune beneath the ocean and Satan beneath the earth. Thus, in spite of the potentially destructive nature of this symbol, in a dream the trident indicates that unconscious material is emerging into consciousness. This is not inherently bad. In fact, it is a sign of progress and integration of the personality.

TRIP (*see* JOURNEY)

TRIPOD

Any tripod, from stool to surveying tool, represents a stable structure. In a dream it reminds us of the sun's movement from dawn to midday to sunset. It thus represents swift movement as well as stability. The child's tricycle is an example of the capacity for human constructions to allow for greater mobility.

TRIUMPH

Triumph in a dream symbolizes power.

TROUT (*see* SALMON)

TRUMPET

Trumpets and horns symbolize nobility or even divinity. They engender these qualities in you or in other dream figures with which they are associated.

TUNIC (see CLOTHES, SHIRT)

TUNNEL (see HALLWAY)

TURKEY
The founding fathers of the United States considered making the turkey the national bird, but decided on the eagle instead. That the turkey was considered shows its importance to the American Indians and to the colonists. A turkey in your dream symbolizes the richness of your harvest, and indicates you have been successful is some area of your life.

TURQUOISE
Ranging in color from green to robin's egg blue, the stone turquoise contains impurities that give it its depth of character and monetary value. The stone is used by American Indians to make jewelry for decoration and also as a show of wealth. The stone represents healing properties and is often associated with the heart or heart chakra. Its clarity of sky colors suggests that intellectual objectivity is of value when it appears in a dream.

TURTLE (TORTOISE)
The turtle is patient, steadfast, and earthy. In stories the tortoise defeats the hare through consistent effort. It symbolizes the material plane and its reality for you. The processes of practical awareness and evaluation are called for. No amount of pushing is effective when the turtle appears. Let things work out in their own good time. Focus on the practical for the time being.

TURTLEDOVE
The turtledove symbolizes love.

TWILIGHT (HALF-LIGHT)
Twilight or half-light symbolizes the dichotomy of day and night. In a dream it may signal a dichotomy between dream elements of which you have been unaware in consciousness.

TWINS (DUALISM) (see also DOUBLE)
Twins and other doubles share a Trickster nature and serve to alert you to dual meanings in the dream.

TWISTED THINGS
Twisted or bent objects imply that some force of nature has been used to shape them. Their abnormal shape may be cause for concern, or it may simply indicate that some processes require this kind of force. Screws are one such object in which twisting is part of their nature.

Two

Two symbolizes diversity, reflection, and conflict. It implies growth and the passage of time. One comes before, and is less than, two. Two is suggestive of all life processes. It also suggests the intuitive process of mind.

u

Umbrella (*see* Sunshade)

Undines

Undines and other water nymphs are symbols of the feminine. They also symbolize the unknown, and therefore treacherous, nature of the unconscious. When they appear in a dream they invite you to examine unconscious information that is being provided.

Unicorn

When a unicorn appears in a dream, it recalls the purity and grace of the mythical animal. It is thought to be able to escape all things but will submit to a virgin. What in your life has the purity of the unicorn? What are you seeking to purify? Is there a pure feeling or thought that you feel needs to escape capture or be protected? The unicorn is thought to live as long as a thousand years, and thus may represent something that is enduring in your life experience.

Urine (Pee)

Dreaming of urinating is often a signal that you actually need to visit the bathroom. It also symbolizes the catharsis of eliminating a feeling or thought that is no longer needed. It can signal the possibility of refocusing on something more meaningful in the present by letting go of the past.

Urn

The urn symbolizes containment. It is a feminine symbol. The Chinese felt that an urn with a lid was a symbol of good luck, and also the fuller consciousness we attain after death. In a dream it can indicate the feminine aspect of the dream, good fortune, or intelligence that is offered by a guide or spirit to you.

Utensils

Utensils symbolize the genius of human beings to extend their reach and to work with the environment.

v

VAGINA (*see* **GENITALIA**)

VALLEY
Valleys are characteristically fertile places because water flows into them carrying dissolved minerals. In dreams the valley symbolizes life forces at work.

VASE
Because it is a container, the vase symbolizes the feminine in general.

VAULT
Whether it is a pole vault at a sports event or a bank vault, the word relates to the vault of heaven—the canopy of the sky. It symbolizes the connection between earth and heaven, or between man and spirit.

VEGETATION
Vegetation can serve to symbolize the season of the year based on its condition and size. It also symbolizes fertility and growth, and therefore may symbolize general health.

VEHICLES
All vehicles can be viewed as reflections of the body. In your dream the vehicle and its condition say something about you and your overall state of health and happiness.

VEIL
A veiled person or object in a dream is hidden from your view. This may occur so you will not be too startled by what you see and cause you to awake before the dream is complete. Also, the veil serves to conceal something about your inner self.

VENUS
The planet Venus is closest to Earth's size than any other planet, yet its surface conditions are unlivable. Acid rain and extreme heat makes life there very unlikely. In esoteric lore this planet is the alter ego of the Earth. The goddess is a metaphor for the perfect feminine, and symbolizes perfect spiritual love as well as sexual attraction.

VERTICAL SPACES
Vertical spaces symbolize the ascent of the moral or spiritual being to states of "greater good."

VICTORY
Victory, whether personified as a winged figure, or felt as a sense of accomplishment in the dream, symbolizes the conquest of a psychological or spiritual adversary or a challenge.

VINE

Vines symbolize youth and eternal life of the spirit.

VIOLET

The color violet often represents the alpha brain wave rhythm associated with a relaxed, meditative state. It represents a transition from red to blue, and relates to memory. It may also stand for the flower, which is shy and retiring.

VIRGO

The sixth sign of the zodiac is sometimes represented by Isis or other feminine figures. This sign symbolizes the harvest, and the integration of opposite forces.

VIRTUES (*see* ANGELS)

VOID (*see* ABYSS, EMPTINESS, MACROCOSM, NOTHINGNESS, SPACE)

VOLCANO

A volcano symbolizes the destructive forces within the psyche. It is the natural analog of pent-up rage finally exploding. It represents all our passions.

VULCAN

The god Vulcan symbolizes the creative force of God or the gods, and as such also represents ultimate spiritual energy.

VULTURE

The vulture is an ominous bird that circles above something dead or that is about to die. It is therefore a dark symbol of the end of some cycle of experience. The positive expression of the vulture is a clear field that allows something else to take the place of an old, dead idea or feeling. The Egyptians associated the vulture with the energy of Mother Nature who gives life and then takes it back into herself.

W

WALL

A wall is a barrier. It can symbolize a barrier against the elements if it is part of a house, or it can serve as a fence between two areas. In a dream the wall may be an obstacle that needs to be climbed over (rising above the problem), dug under (seeking inner illumination of the problem), or bypassed (taking a practical approach to the problem). One can go through a wall either by destroying the wall or by finding a doorway through it, symbolizing the process of finding the solution within the problem itself.

WALLOWING

Animals wallow in the mud or water to protect their skin from the sun and from insects. In a dream wallowing may seem messy, but you may want to consider the need to take time to protect your psyche from some onslaught of energy in your life.

WAND (*see also* SCEPTER)

The user energizes the wand over time. The wand is used to direct psychic energy. In a dream the wand signals a way for you to direct your energies effectively.

WANDERING JEW

This plant is a symbol of the immortal wanderer or pilgrim. It symbolizes the immortal soul.

WAR (BATTLE)

A war or battle in a dream symbolizes the forces of light and darkness (the polarized elements of any problem). The more vigorous the action of the battle, the more you understand that your inner struggle is active.

WARRIORS

The people who inhabit a battle or who prepare for war in a dream symbolize the innate strengths you have gathered during your life. Even hostile forces symbolize part of your inner being.

WASH (*see* CANYON)

WATER (*see also* DELUGE, OCEAN, RAIN, RAINBOW, REEFS, RIVER, WAVE, WETNESS)

Water is the matter from which the world was made at the time of Creation. Water symbolizes life. Its condition reflects something about the way you see life at any given time.

WAVE (*see also* DELUGE, OCEAN, RAIN, RAINBOW, REEFS, RIVER, WATER, WETNESS)

The wave symbolizes the constantly changing nature of life, movement within the psyche, an d purity. The yin-yang symbol of Taoism is composed of a circle and a wave. The ocean meets land in waves, symbolizing the flow of unconscious material into consciousness. The symbol for the zodiacal sign Aquarius is two waves. The quality of the wave or waves in a dream suggests the emotional significance to you at a particular point in time.

WEAPONS

Weapons in a dream symbolize the qualities of your personality that you bring to a psychic problem.

WEASEL (FERRET)

Quickness and stealth are characteristics of the weasel. It changes its color with the season to make it hard to see. A weasel or ferret in a dream may indicate that you are learning hidden secrets, or that you are yourself hiding something, or can benefit from concealing part of what you know.

WEATHER (*see* **CLIMATE**)

WEAVING (SNARE, WEB)
(*see also* **ENTANGLEMENT, NET, SPIDER, SPIDER WOMAN, SPINNING**)
Weaving is a universal symbol for the creative forces of life. It also symbolizes the intelligence behind the pattern.

WEB (*see* **ENTANGLEMENT, NET, SPIDER, SPIDER WOMAN, SPINNING, WEAVING**)

WEEK
A week, as displayed on a calendar or date book, symbolizes the passage of a short period of time.

WELL
The well symbolizes a deep source of psychic strength and also a connection to the collective mind. It replenishes and nourishes the psyche according to the quality of water in it.

WEST
West is the direction of the future. If you travel west in your dream, you are getting a glimpse of things to come.

WETNESS (SOLUTION)
(*see also* **DELUGE, OCEAN, RAIN, RAINBOW, REEFS, RIVER, WATER, WAVE**)
Any wet place or object in your dream indicates the alchemical function of *solutio,* or dissolving the *prima materia* to purify it. This involves a journey into unconscious realms. The place or object is a cue to go deeper, or it may be a clue to the information you seek.

WHALE
The whale is the largest of animals, and therefore represents a large feeling or thought. It lives in water and surfaces to breathe, just as unconscious and archetypal material resides in the unconscious and comes to the surface to inform you about some facet of your life. The one way to interpret a whale in a dream is that it is a large idea coming from deep within yourself. Living in water but breathing air, the whale symbolizes opposites of unconscious and conscious mind, and possibly any set of opposites you may encounter. It may signal you to look for the opposing viewpoint in a situation.

WHEEL

The wheel has two principal meanings. First, it is part of a means of transportation, and thus represents the capacity to move quickly in the dream. Second, it is a mandala (a circle with a center), and thus symbolizes wholeness. Movement via wheeled vehicles in a dream therefore can symbolize movement toward wholeness.

WHEEL OF FORTUNE

In tarot, the wheel is the tenth card of the Major Arcana and symbolizes constant change. It incorporates both progressive and recessive movement, both constructive and destructive activity. The wheel itself symbolizes wholeness, and this card indicates that both sides of any situation contribute to eventual self-awareness.

WHIP

The whip is an instrument of control through pain. It symbolizes domination and superiority based on physical power.

WHIRLPOOL (see BREEZE, HURRICANE, WIND)

WHIRLWIND (see BREEZE, HURRICANE, WIND)

WHISTLING

Whistling symbolizes calling upon a guide, spirit, or deity for help.

WHITE

The color white is associated with purity in alchemy and connected with the Ascension of Christ (and other religious figures). It is sometimes associated with pardons and also the appearance of deities to human beings. White reflects spiritual purity and also innocence.

WILD MAN/WILD WOMAN

A wild man or woman symbolizes the instinctual part of your personality. It may be offering information that you have forgotten or are ignoring about the basics of your inner nature. It is possible that the wilder they are, the more distant you are from some central principles of yourself. At the same time they may lead you on an adventure during which you discover these inner values.

WIND (CYCLONE, TORNADO, WHIRLPOOL, WHIRLWIND) (see also BREEZE, HURRICANE)

Any movement of air indicates the alchemical process of *sublimatio,* or rising above the material world to gain objectivity. It implies that the thinking process—the logical use of intellect—is required.

WINDOW

The window symbolizes the eye, and therefore the window of the soul, and also consciousness. Multiple panes of glass or windows close together may symbolize the number of factors at play in the dream and how they relate to each other. Rational thinking is needed to establish and understand the relationships.

WINE

Beyond the obvious symbolism of intoxication, wine has been used to symbolize blood and its life-giving properties, and also sacrifice.

WINGS

Wings symbolize several things. First they symbolize spirituality. They also represent thought or imagination—the capacity to engage the mind. They symbolize flight in the air, and also the ability to remove oneself from a situation literally or figuratively.

WINTER

Winter is a season for gathering forces. After the winter solstice sap begins to run in trees, and other hidden functions of nature begin to turn away from the cold of the season toward the warmth of spring. The cold of winter is analogous to the cold, aloof, calculating personality. Thus a dream image in a winter setting may feel insensitive to your needs.

WISE (OLD AGE, WISDOM)

Old people and things in dreams often symbolize wisdom in some way. Examine the character or object for the wisdom it is offering you.

WITHDRAWAL

Leaving the stage or withdrawing from something in a dream has the obvious meaning of saying "no" to some portion of the dream. It also suggests that one of the choices in the situation is to leave the situation. Money leaves the bank account when it is withdrawn, and in a dream this may mean gathering the resources you need to accomplish a task. Both leaving the stage and withdrawing from an account symbolize the decision-making capacity.

WOLF (*see also* APOLLO)

The wolf can be a silent ally in a dream or an indication that you are on a path seeking something greater than yourself. The wolf is a guide, leading you to your psychic treasure. The wolf is a teacher, then, able to show you something valuable when you call upon it. If it appears in your dream then perhaps you have been actively seeking psychic insights. The wolf's role is similar to the role of family members who lead you in the process of development, offer protection, but at the same time challenge you to move forward into your own leadership role. The wolf represents a teacher.

WOMAN

A female figure in a dream symbolizes some aspect of the anima, in addition to any other role she plays. Aspects of the feminine archetype include the Daughter, the Mother, and the Crone—the three distinct roles at different stages of life. Another view suggests Enchantress, Mother, and Unknown Damsel.

WOMB (*see* GENITALIA)

WOOD

Wood symbolizes the natural in a dream. The quality and texture of it are clues to the direction you may take to regain a more natural sense of self. It also symbolizes the fire of intuition, but in a latent, expectant state.

WOODPECKER

The woodpecker is industrious as it creates its home and searches for food by tapping away at trees or the side of a house. Its sound can be irritating and divert your attention from an absorbing task. Or the rhythm can be soothing and remind you of the value of repetitive actions. The feeling you had when the woodpecker appeared is significant. If it irritates you, then perhaps it is trying to draw your attention to something you have overlooked. If it is soothing, perhaps it is reminding you of the internal rhythms of the body and mind that provide continuity and comfort. It may symbolize the ordinariness of something with which it is associated in your dream.

WORLD

The world may symbolize wholeness of the personality. It also represents the social sphere.

In tarot, card twenty-one of the Major Arcana is the World and symbolizes the result of creative activity. It suggests that the outcome of your activities will be successful.

WORM

Worms are primitive; they live in damp, dark places and seldom come to the surface. A worm may remind you of death and dissolution. At the same time it is full of the basic energy of life as it wriggles its way along. In this sense it symbolizes the fertility of the dream situation. In a dream the worm's path may be worth examining. Where has it been and where is it going?

X-Ray

Just as the x-ray pictures the solid structures of the body, it symbolizes the solid, inner spiritual map. In a dream an x-ray may point to a part of the body that needs attention, or it may be a metaphorical indication of an emotional, mental, or spiritual need.

Yang (*see* Yin)

Yard

The yard around a house symbolizes, by its degree of cultivation, the civilizing influence you provide in the dream situation.

Year (Calendar)

A calendar or the season's cycle reminds you of the passage of a year's time and thus symbolizes the seasons of one's life.

Yellow

The color yellow reflects the farsighted function of intuition. In Buddhism it reflects the capacity to reach out and embrace everything. Yellow is associated with the emperor of China and is the color of the solar plexus chakra.

Yin (Yang)

Yin and yang are, respectively, the feminine and masculine principles that join together to form the symbol of the Tao. Within each principle is the seed of the other as represented by the dots in the yin-yang symbol. This and similar symbols remind us of the duality of everything in nature. The symbol may be inviting you to consider the balance in the dream and in your waking life.

Yoke

The yoke that connects a team of working animals symbolizes the union of two or more things into a working unit. It also suggests the discipline of the team. The yoke on a garment is so named because it resembles the part of the harness and thus shares the same symbolic meaning.

YONI

The yoni, often depicted as an almond-shaped design or a stylized vulva, is the gateway between the material and spiritual realms—between ascent and descent, or life and death. The intersection of these energies symbolizes the creative force of the universe. The lingam is the masculine counterpart to the yoni.

YOUTH

Masculine figures of youth and old age symbolize, respectively, the sun in its rising and setting. As such these figures together symbolize the movement of time. A young figure symbolizes a fresh idea or feeling. What are the feelings you associate with youth or newness in your dream?

YULE (CHRISTMAS)

The celebrations of deep winter symbolize the sun's expected return to the Northern Hemisphere as the year progresses toward spring. Decoration with ornaments and lights symbolize the sun's rekindling fire, a ceremony that is practiced in many religions. Decorated tree branches were sometimes used for protection during the days immediately following the winter solstice.

ZENITH

The zenith is the highest point in the sky, directly overhead. While for most of us the sun is never in this position, in a dream this point may symbolize the sun at its highest point at noon. The zenith in the sky symbolizes the high point of some activity you are engaged in.

ZERO

The number zero represents nonbeing, but it is also a placeholder in our number system. Zero's circular nature reflects the quality of the mandala and also of eternity.

ZIGGURAT

This Sumerian pyramid-shaped temple symbolizes the mountain that emerged during the creation from the waters.

ZODIAC

The zodiac symbolizes the process of life from a sprouting seed to harvest to decay to dormancy.

Dream Tutorial

The dream tutorial in the CD-ROM program follows the basic format of the following list of questions, and includes some prompts to help you identify significant qualities in your dream. You may want to use this outline when you first begin to record your dreams. Later you may find that you have a personal rhythm that allows you to get the most out of each dream you record.

1. How does the dream start?
2. Describe the dream setting.
3. Where are you?
4. How are you dressed?
5. What are you doing in the dream? (or not doing?)
6. What other characters are present at the beginning? Do you know them? Describe how they look, how they are dressed, and so on.
7. What happens after that?
8. Does the dream have an ending? Is there anything you notice that is left unresolved?
9. How do you feel when you wake up?
10. How do you feel when you are recording the dream?
11. Are you aware of any connections between the dream and your waking life?
12. What most attracts you in the dream? Why?
13. What do you wish to avoid in the dream? Why?
14. Is there a helper or guide in the dream? How do you relate to it?

15. Imagine that the characters in the dream are part of you. How do you feel about them being you?

16. Imagine the places and actions being part of you. How does that make you feel?

17. What things in the dream stand out as being the most important to you? Why?

18. Does this dream relate to other dreams you recall?

19. What have you learned from the dream so far?

20. Title of the dream.

21. Date of dream. (This will be generated by the computer's clock but you can change it.)

22. Can you categorize the dream? What kind of dream is it?

Sample Dream Tutorial

1. How does the dream start?
   I am in the desert.

2. Describe the dream setting.
   It is night, actually just before dawn.

3. Where are you?
   I am outside a low, dome-shaped building. There is a sort of totem pole object that turns into a saguaro cactus and back again.

4. How are you dressed?
   I don't see myself, so I don't know. My legs and arms are bare, though.

5. What are you doing in the dream? (or not doing?)
   I am waiting for the sun to rise. I can see its light striking the mountains to my west, but it is not yet visible in the east.

6. What other characters are present at the beginning? Do you know them? Describe how they look, how they are dressed, and so on.
   I am the only person at the beginning of the dream.

7. What happens after that?
   The sun rises and I enter the building through a low doorway. Inside there is darkness, but I can "see" because of a bluish light vibration. I sit on a low seat or

cushion. There is a fire near the east wall and two other seats. There has been a fire, but there is no smoke now.

Two other people come into the building. One is a woman who controls water energy and the other is a man who controls earth energy. I hold the fire energy. The fire itself (which is now lit) has sage or pinion in it. The smoke represents air energy.

I melt into the smoke and follow it up through a hole in the ceiling. I spread out on the smoke as far as it will go, and I can see a distant village below. There is a black thought form there. As I watch, the thought form spreads out and its energy dissolves. I come back into the hut and am back in my physical body.

8. Does the dream have an ending? Is there anything you notice that is left unresolved?

   There is more to the dream, but this part of it feels complete at this point.

9. How do you feel when you wake up?

   Happy and rested.

10. How do you feel when you are recording the dream?

    Spreading out on the air has a feeling of tremendous freedom. I can do it without disappearing, the way the black thought form did. I am witnessing the process of death, but I do not die.

11. Are you aware of any connections between the dream and your waking life?

    I work with the basic elements in astrology and other areas of my life.

12. What most attracts you in the dream? Why?

    The anticipation of the sunrise, the ability to rise up out of my body.

13. What do you wish to avoid in the dream? Why?

    The black thought form. It is filled with the fears of the people in the village.

14. Is there a helper or guide in the dream? How do you relate to it?

    The man and woman are my guides. They anchor me so that I can go out of my body safely.

15. Imagine that the characters in the dream are part of you. How do you feel about them being you?

    I can be my own anchor—ground myself when I am experiencing something new or scary.

16. Imagine the places and actions being part of you. How does that make you feel?

    Floating seems like a time-wasting activity, yet it is so comfortable to be able to do this. Making the thought form dissolve is very satisfying. The desert is something I feel in my blood all the time. I think it is the spaciousness that calls to me. The mountains call also. For the first part of my life I could always see a 14,000-foot peak from my house.

17. What things in the dream stand out as being the most important to you? Why?

    The ritual of meeting the sunrise before an important activity seems the most important. Preparing in the proper way for any activity.

18. Does this dream relate to other dreams you recall?

    No.

19. What have you learned from the dream so far?

    That I am a powerful person, and that my powers are different from other people around me. I learned these powers in a past lifetime, and can use them again now.

20. Title of the dream.

    Rising Up on the Smoke

21. Date of dream. (This will be generated by the computer's clock but you can change it.)

    October 26, 1988

22. Can you categorize the dream? What kind of dream is it?

    Waking vision, lucid, balancing

User Manual

Welcome to *Dreams: Working Interactive,* your interactive dream journaling program. Llewellyn Worldwide, Terry, and I all hope you enjoy this approach to tracking your dream and visionary life, and look forward to your comments and suggestions. Llewellyn and Terry and I also look forward to your contributions of interesting dreams and new symbols. We will consider all submissions for addition to our symbol dictionary, so please share with us! If we accept your submissions for publication, your entries will be documented with your name and email address, or with a pseudonym. You can, of course, request to remain anonymous and still get your ideas into the book or dictionary.

Installation

For Windows 95, 98, and NT. Insert the CD into the CD-ROM drive and follow the directions that appear on the screen. Read the "Readme.txt" file under the Help drop-down menu for additional useful information before beginning.

Registration

Please take the time to fill out the registration form in the back of the book and either email it to Llewellyn Worldwide or print it and mail it in. Llewellyn will use the information you provide to notify you of updates to the program and the dream dictionary.

Using the Program

When the program first opens, you see a screen in which you can enter a new dream or new dreamer. The program allows an unlimited number of household members to use the same program and there is no limit to the number of dreams that can be entered.

The program will prevent you from creating duplicate dream titles. The disadvantage of this is that you have to "dream up" a new title for each dream. The advantage is that the program reminds you of a similar dream you have had before.

Dream Entry

The first time you use the program, a default dreamer and dream will appear in the windows on the screen. You will want to enter a name for yourself into the program. The name of the first dream cannot be changed.

You can enter a new name by clicking on the Add Dreamer button. A dialogue box will appear with a blank where you can fill in your name. Click "Done" to go back to the Dream Entry page and to add the name to the dreamer list. Click "Cancel" to exit the window without adding a new name.

Each time you use the program, you can select your dreamer name from the Dreamer Name drop-down menu in the upper right-hand part of the Dream Entry screen. If you create more than one name for yourself, select any name and then enter a new dream.

Follow the same basic procedure of entering a new dreamer name to enter the name of your dream. Click on the Add Dream button and the New Dream Entry window will appear. In the first box, today's date is automatically entered by your computer's clock. In the second box, enter the date you had the dream. (If it is different from today's date, enter the correct date.) In the third box you can enter a title for the dream. Each of the boxes has a default entry, which you can change by highlighting the contents of the window and typing over them. Use the Done button to create your new dream file, or the Cancel button to exit without creating a new dream file.

To record the dream itself you have several options:

1. You can highlight all the words in the Dream Entry window for the first dream and write over them. You can type as much as you want. For subsequent dreams, the entry window will be blank. Just click in the window and begin typing.

2. You may want to type your dream in a word processing program, where you can do a spell and grammar check and reformat your writing. You can use the cut and paste protocols of Windows to copy the dream into the Dream Entry window from your other program.

3. The dream program includes a tutorial file that can help you learn about dream journaling. If you want to use this file, to record your dream, do the following:

   a. Using the file drop-down menu, go to open the file. The default file is a dream tutorial. Click "Open" to move the tutorial into the dream entry window. Any .txt document can be moved into the dream window in this way.

   b. Enter your dream or respond to each of the questions or suggestions. If you recall more information about the dream, you will be able to scroll back up and add it where you want it to appear.

At the bottom of the Dream Entry page there is a place to record short notes (256 characters or less) about the dream. Add longer notes to the dream text itself. You might want to use the Notes window to:

1. Mention other dreams that seem related to this one.

2. Mention events in your waking life that relate to the dream that you don't want to include within the dream itself.

3. Mention any other associations you have to the dream.

When you have completed your dream entry, you can either:

1. Click on "Save and Analyze." This choice takes you to the Dream Analysis window, where you can see the dictionary words that have been recorded in the dream.

2. Click on "Save Dream." This saves the dream to the database.

3. Use the File drop-down menu and go to "Save Dream" to save your dream to a .txt file in any folder you choose.

4. Click on "Exit." This erases anything you have written and does not save it to the program's database. It allows you to exit from the program.

5. Use the File drop-down menu and go to Print Report to access the Print Report dialog box.

Color Options

In the Options drop-down menu you can select display colors. If you are familiar with color selection from other programs, you will recognize the Color dialog box that appears when you click each new color button. In the dialog box you have forty-eight colors to choose from and a grouping of spaces for the creation of custom colors. These basic colors provide a range of options that work for most people. Each time you choose a color and use the OK button, you will go back to the color selection screen, and you will be able to see a sample of what you have chosen in the box on the right side of that screen. For help with the Color dialog box, click on "?" in the upper right-hand corner of the box. The click on the item you want help with.

By working with the Color dialog box you can choose just about any color. This takes some practice, so at first you may want to select colors from the basic color palette.

The buttons on the Color Selection screen include selections for:

- Background color
- Text box background
- Words in text boxes
- Buttons throughout the program
- Color of highlighted words from the dream dictionary
- Color of highlighted words from the custom dictionary

Pay close attention to the colors you choose, as you want to be able to read the words against their backgrounds. Each time you use a selection button and choose a color, the right side of the screen will show you what you have selected.

At the bottom of the screen are the following buttons:

- Terry's Favorites and Stephanie's Favorites: We have included our favorites, in case you want to choose a set of colors quickly.

- Default Colors: This button accesses your color selections from the operating system, so that *Dreams: Working Interactive* will have the same appearance as your other programs. Dream dictionary and custom dictionary words here are the same color.

- Apply: This button applies the colors and leaves you in the Color dialog box so you can continue to make changes.

- Cancel: Use the Cancel button to leave this part of the program and return to the Dream Entry page.
- When you are finished, use the OK button to apply the colors throughout the program and return to the program.

Dream Analysis Window

Use the Save and Analyze button on the Dream Entry page to go to the Dream Analysis window. You will see your dream in the upper left-hand box. In the lower left is the definition of the first symbol highlighted in your dream. In the upper right is a list of symbols that occur in both your dream and the dream dictionary. You can go through this list and uncheck any of the symbols that you do not wish to appear in your completed dream analysis report. Eliminate the embedded words if they don't make any sense in the context of your dream. Simply use your mouse to click on the check box next to the word and remove the check mark from the box.

In the lower right-hand corner is a custom symbol window. Here you will find words that you have added to your custom dream dictionary. (For instructions on how to add to your custom dream dictionary, see below.) As you click on each word in either the dream dictionary or your custom list, the definition in the lower left window changes. (Note: If a word is in both dictionaries, it will be highlighted in the color associated with the dream dictionary list.)

To save your dream and highlighted symbols to a file, use the File drop-down menu and go to Save. Then use the Windows save protocols to save your dream to the output folder (default) or other Windows folder. This will *not* save the symbol definitions.

Use the Print button to go to the Print Report screen where you can choose printing options and print the dream.

Each time you analyze the dream, you will be able to change the word selections. These selections are not saved. Print out the dream to create a permanent record.

Use the Exit button to return to the Dream Entry page.

Dictionary

The Dictionary page can be accessed from the Options drop-down menu in the Dream Entry window. On this page you can use the program's dictionary to look up words and read their meanings. You can also look up custom words that you have added to the dictionary.

To use the dream dictionary or the custom dictionary, scroll through the list and click on the word to highlight it. The associated meaning will appear in the box to the right of the list. Scroll through the meaning if it is larger than the box.

Use the Exit button to return to the Dream Entry page.

Custom Word Entry

From the Dictionary dialog box, use the Add New Word button to access the Custom Word Entry dialog box. In this box you can add words to your dream program that are not in the dictionary, or you can add your own definition of a word that is already in the dictionary. In this way you retain the symbol definitions supplied with the program while augmenting them with your own personalized meanings. But if you're sharing this program with others, be sure to add only personal definitions you are willing to share with your dream partners. All custom words and definitions will appear in the Dream Analysis window.

To add a word, type the word in the word box. If you already have a word with the same spelling in your custom dictionary, the program will tell you. Then you can re-enter the word with a different definition. You will then have two custom definitions come up in the next dream that includes the word "house." You can have multiple definitions for any one word.

When you are satisfied with what you have written, use the Add to Dictionary button to complete your entry and save it. If you enter a word and then decide to remove it from the dictionary, you can use the word list to find the word, check to see that what is in the window is the correct word, and then use the Delete Word button. You will not be able to delete words from the dream dictionary.

If you decide to quit without adding the word, use the Done Editing button to return to the previous screen. Use the Clear Contents button to erase and start over.

You can enter any word you wish, and then create your own definition of the symbol. This option has two possibilities:

1. You can add a symbol that is not already in the dictionary. As mentioned earlier, you can send these definitions to Llewellyn Worldwide who will consider adding them to the standard dream dictionary for other people to share what you have discovered.

2. You can make notes about recurring dream images, characters, or especially significant aspects of your dream. Then if the same word is used in a later dream, the "definition" will serve as a reminder of the earlier dream. In this way you can track characters, images, and so on through your customized dictionary.

Print Report

You can access the Print Report screen through the Dream Analysis page by using the Print/Save Report button. On this page you find options for printing that determine how your dream will look, and what information will appear in the printout. There are five check boxes that allow you to select the following for inclusion:

- Personal Data: This includes the name and date associated with the dream. If you have more than one user, or more than one index for yourself, you will want to print this information.
- Dream Text: You will probably always want to check this box so that the dream itself appears in the printout.
- List of Found Words: You may not need this list in all cases, but it can be a helpful quick reference to the symbol definitions in the dream.
- Words with Their Definitions: You may not need this section all the time, but often you will want the dream and its associated symbol definitions together.
- Dream Notes: If there are no notes, then you probably won't check this box. If the notes are private and you are printing the dream for general use, you might want to omit this information. For your own personal use, you will probably want to include any notes you have made.

On the right side of the screen are five buttons that help you to complete the printing task:

- Print: This will print all the items you have selected from the check list.
- Select All: This selects all five items on the check list.
- Clear All: This clears all the items so you can begin again.
- Save to File: You may want to save the entire report to the output folder in the Dreams program folder. It will be saved as an RTF file which you can later

open in a word processing program to edit, reformat the printing, or read. This will *not* highlight the dictionary words within the dream. It will save the words and their definitions separately.

- Exit: This button takes you back to the Dream Analysis page.

At the bottom of this window you can select the appearance of your printout:

- Font Options: You can select the type size you want from the selection box.
- Heading and body text: Use the up and down arrows in the text boxes to change the font size, or type the font size in the boxes.

Remember, you can enter dreams, visions, and diary entries into the program, all of which will be analyzed. Use the Help menu in the program if you have questions. Questions and answers about this program will periodically be added the Llewellyn website at www.llewellyn.com or you can email technical support at dreams@llewellyn.com. Now you are on your way to happy journaling!

Glossary

ARCHETYPE—Nothing is a definitive archetype. Plato may have spoken about the archetypal chair, but when it comes right down to it, we all know what a chair is, and we can identify furniture by their appropriate names. Yet we also know that not all chairs have four legs, or spindles on the back, or arms. The term *archetype* is used to describe objects or concepts upon which there is broad, possibly even global agreement. Within that agreement there is room for an infinite number of variations, and each of us has our own take on the archetypal content of our lives.

Everyone's dreams pursue archetypes, whether we are aware of it or not, because we are fascinated with these larger-than-life ideas. When a dream element has a life of its own aside from the content of the dream, when it is "alive" with feelings, then you know that an archetype is being evoked. You will often find that some problem in your waking life appears to be caused by your pursuit of the archetype. Paradoxically, it is this energy that can provide the solution to the problem if you allow the archetype to develop naturally.

BINARY—Any binary symbol reflects the dual quality of physical experience, as well as the dual nature of the conscious and unconscious minds. To perceive wholeness, duality is necessary; yet to appreciate the wholeness or oneness of the world is a source of spiritual certainty.

CLAIRAUDIENCE—The capacity to hear sounds that are not within the ordinary range of hearing. This could involve ordinary words spoken hundreds of miles away from you, or it could involve the apprehension of a voice from the astral or spiritual planes.

COMPENSATION—An adjustment within a dream to reflect the dreamer's conscious opinion concerning a dream element. Such an adjustment can be in either a positive or negative direction.

DAIMON—The spirit within each of us is a unique expression of the mind. This spirit guides us through life. While it may seem silent at times, it never gives up trying to help us be our very best.

EIDETIC—An eidetic memory is recalled in such total detail that it is more vivid in some ways than it seemed when it first occurred. This is especially true of visual content, but could extend to hearing, smell, or touch. Certain dreams have an eidetic quality, and thus stand out from the rest and are remembered easily.

ENANTIODROMIA—A play of opposites. Two symbols of opposite natures may occur in a dream to point out a fallacy in thinking or a dilemma you are facing in the dream or in your waking life.

INDIVIDUATION—This developmental process continues throughout your life. It is the goal of the daimon or spirit to help you achieve the best you possibly can and achieve wholeness of personality. Individuation is the spontaneous recognition of the whole self, and replaces the tendency to view life from the perspective of one complex of thoughts and feelings to the exclusion of others.

MANDALA—The simplest mandala is a circle with a center. This is a symbol of wholeness found throughout all cultures. It often has divisions of four, or eight, or twelve, and so on, and sometimes is a square within the circle or a circle within the square.

NUMINOUS—Supernatural or mysterious, filled with a sense of the divine, spiritual. An object filled with numinosity may be said to have a spell attached to it. The psychic content of such an object makes it sacred in nature. Spiritual mystery exists not only for the individual dreamer, but on a collective (archetypal) level. The power of a numinous image is, at least at first, unconscious, and understanding the power brings the individual into harmony with a larger reality. The power of a magical implement, an idol, or the image of a saint lies in its imbued numinosity or psychic energy.

Bibliography

Andrews, Ted. *Animal-Speak*. St. Paul: Llewellyn, 1993.

Argüelles, Jose, and Miriam Argüelles. *Mandala*. Berkeley and London: Shambhala, 1972.

Bennet, E. A. *What Jung Really Said*. New York: Schocken Books, 1967.

Case, Paul Foster. *The Book of Tokens: 22 Meditations on the Ageless Wisdom*. Los Angeles: Builders of the Adytum, 1934.

Cirlot, J. E. *A Dictionary of Symbols*. New York: Philosophical Library, 1971.

Jung, C. G. *Dreams*. Princeton, N.J.: Princeton University Press, 1974.

Randles, Jenny. *Time Travel: Fact, Fiction & Possibility*. London: Blandford, 1994.

Shelley, Percy Bysshe. *The Works of Percy Bysshe Shelley*. New York: Black's Readers Service by special arrangement with Random House, 1951.

Slemen, Thomas. *Strange but True: Mysterious and Bizarre People*. New York: Barnes & Noble, 1998.

Sun Bear, and Wabun Wind. *Dreaming with the Wheel*. New York: Fireside, 1994.

Williams, Strephon Kaplan. *Jungian-Senoi Dreamwork Manual*. Berkeley: Journey Press, 1980.

Index

archetype, x, 3, 8-9, 21, 36, 54, 62, 72, 104, 112, 120, 124, 128, 130, 139, 150, 152, 167, 169, 191, 197, 200, 215-216

centering, 9-10, 172
Cirlot, 17, 66, 126
complex, 4-5, 68, 84, 116, 216
creativity, 5, 11, 40-41, 57, 66-67, 69, 77-79, 83, 88, 92, 96, 101-102, 104, 117, 131-132, 143, 145-147, 149-152, 154, 156, 169, 175-176, 178-181, 184, 186, 195, 197, 200, 202

daimon, 16-18, 38, 175, 216
Dalai Lama, 50

enantiodromia, 34, 216

flight, 89, 129, 199
Forbidden City, 28
Freud, Sigmund, 8, 66, 68, 118, 126, 130

golden mean, 121, 183

individuation, ix, 68, 137, 216

Joan of Arc, 28-29
Jung, Carl, ix, 3, 8, 23, 66-67, 69, 128

Keller, Helen, 21
Kennedy, John F., Jr., 49, 72

mana, 66, 128
mandala, 80, 88-89, 100-101, 111, 122, 125, 147, 198, 202, 216

Nebuchadnezzar, 35-37, 62, 72
numinosity, 27, 168, 216

penis, 65-66, 126, 162
phallus, 66-67, 146, 163

ritual, 10-12, 28, 66, 129, 170, 179, 183-184, 187, 206

Shekinah, 180
Shelley, Percy Bysshe, 49-50, 72-73
Swedenborg, Emanuel, 51, 53-54
symbol systems, 12

☾ REACH FOR THE MOON

Llewellyn publishes hundreds of books on your favorite subjects!
To get these exciting books, including the ones on the following pages,
check your local bookstore or order them directly from Llewellyn.

Order by Phone

- Call toll-free within the U.S. and Canada, 1-800-THE MOON
- In Minnesota, call (651) 291-1970
- We accept VISA, MasterCard, and American Express

Order by Mail

- Send the full price of your order (MN residents add 7% sales tax) in U.S. funds, plus postage & handling to:

  Llewellyn Worldwide
  P.O. Box 64383, Dept. K145-7
  St. Paul, MN 55164-0383, U.S.A.

Postage & Handling

(For the U.S., Canada, and Mexico)

- $4.00 for orders $15.00 and under
- $5.00 for orders over $15.00
- No charge for orders over $100.00

We ship UPS in the continental United States. We ship standard mail to P.O. boxes. Orders shipped to Alaska, Hawaii, the Virgin Islands, and Puerto Rico are sent first-class mail. Orders shipped to Canada and Mexico are sent surface mail.

International orders: Airmail—add freight equal to price of each book to the total price of order, plus $5.00 for each non-book item (audio tapes, etc.).

Surface mail—Add $1.00 per item.

Allow 2 weeks for delivery on all orders.
Postage and handling rates subject to change.

Discounts

We offer a 20% discount to group leaders or agents. You must order a minimum of 5 copies of the same book to get our special quantity price.

Free Catalog

Get a free copy of our color catalog, *New Worlds of Mind and Spirit.* Subscribe for just $10.00 in the United States and Canada ($30.00 overseas, airmail). Many bookstores carry *New Worlds*—ask for it!

Visit our website at www.llewellyn.com for more information.

Charting Your Career
The Horoscope Reveals Your Life Purpose

STEPHANIE JEAN CLEMENT

Clients repeatedly ask astrologers for help with career decisions. *Charting Your Career* provides a unified, elegant, and comprehensive method for analyzing a birth chart and considering the impact of current conditions on career. You will find a fresh approach and new insights, based on the author's psychological and astrological counseling practices.

This book will help you to define your own creativity, see the best path to career success and identify how your skills and life experience fit into the vocational picture. It will help you to understand why your present job is not satisfying, and what you can do to change that. It can help you see where you may have missed opportunities in the past and how to make the most of new ones as they arise. It even shows what kind of building is best for you to work in! Finally, you can see your larger spiritual mission in light of your work abilities.

1-56718-144-9
208 pp., 7½ x 9⅛

$12.95

To order, call 1-800-THE MOON
Prices subject to change without notice

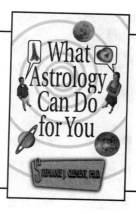

What Astrology Can Do for You
STEPHANIE CLEMENT, PH.D.

So you know your sign, you've read your horoscope in the newspaper, heard all about how Geminis get along great with Leos, and you've skimmed those tabloid predictions. But believe it or not, what you've seen about astrology is just the beginning.

This book opens the door to the real purpose and power of astrology: understanding yourself, your path, and your future.

No two astrological charts are alike, and as you learn about the elements that go into your unique birth chart, you are taking your first steps on a life-long journey to the stars. *What Astrology Can Do for You* will answer the questions:

- Is astrology different from psychic prediction?
- How can I use it to improve my life?
- Can astrology predict a lottery winner?
- How can I figure out what the planets are doing now?
- What signs am I most compatible with?
- What can I forecast using astrology?
- How does it work?
- Is there such as thing as a being born under a "bad sign"?
- What do all these "houses" in my chart mean?
- What about all those triangles and squares in my chart?
- Somebody said I'm on a cusp—what does that mean?
- How long does it really take to learn all this stuff?

1-56718-146-5
192 pp., 4³⁄₁₆ x 6⅞, charts

$4.99

To order, call 1-800-THE MOON
Prices subject to change without notice

Dreams and What They Mean to You
MIGENE GONZÁLEZ-WIPPLER

Everyone dreams. Yet dreams are rarely taken seriously—they seem to be only a bizarre series of amusing or disturbing images that the mind creates for no particular purpose. Yet dreams, through a language of their own, contain essential information about ourselves which, if properly analyzed and understood, can change our lives. In this fascinating and well-written book, the author gives you all of the information needed to begin interpreting—even creating—your own dreams.

Dreams and What They Mean to You begins by exploring the nature of the human mind and consciousness, then discusses the results of the most recent scientific research on sleep and dreams. The author analyzes different types of dreams: telepathic, nightmares, sexual, and prophetic. In addition, there is an extensive Dream Dictionary which lists the meanings for a wide variety of dream images.

Most importantly, González-Wippler tells you how to practice creative dreaming—consciously controlling dreams as you sleep. Once a person learns to control his dreams, his horizons will expand and his chances of success will increase!

0-87542-288-8
240 pp., mass market

$4.99

To order, call 1-800-THE MOON
Prices subject to change without notice

Gypsy Dream Dictionary
(Formerly Secrets of Gypsy Dream Reading. *Now revised and expanded)*

RAYMOND BUCKLAND

The world of dreams is as fascinating as the world of the Gypsies themselves. The Gypsies carried their arcane wisdom and time-tested methods of dream interpretation around the world. Now Raymond Buckland, a descendant of the Romani Gypsies, reveals their fascinating methods. You will learn how to interpret the major symbols and main characters in your dreams to decipher what your subconscious is trying to tell you.

You will also discover how to direct your dreams through "lucid dreaming," the art of doing whatever you want in your dream, as you dream it! Practice astral projecting in your dreams . . . travel to new places or meet with friends at a predetermined location!

1-56718-090-6
240 pp., 5³⁄₁₆ x 6

$7.95

Dreaming the Divine
Techniques for Sacred Sleep

Scott Cunningham

Sleep itself can be a spiritual act. During sleep we enter an alternate state of consciousness in which we're more easily approached by our goddesses and gods. Granted, some dreams do lack deep meaning, but others can lead you to higher states of awareness, provide comfort and counseling, and send warnings of the future.

Dreaming the Divine will show you a unique ritual system designed to secure dreams from your personal deities, based on the techniques of antiquity as well as on personal experience. It also gives you an in-depth guide to remembering and recording your dreams, interpreting them, and determining whether they're of divine origin. The techniques aren't complex—a few simple actions, an invocation, and a bed are all you need.

This book is no less than a guide to a unique form of personal spiritual practice. Based on three millennia of the continuous use of similar rites, it elevates sleep from a necessary period of mental and physical rest to a higher purpose.

1-56718-192-9
260 pp., 5³⁄₁₆ x 8, illus.

$9.95

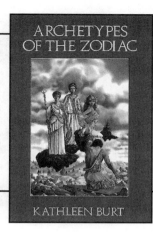

Archetypes of the Zodiac
KATHLEEN BURT

The horoscope is probably the most unique tool for personal growth you can ever have. This book is intended to help you understand how the energies within your horoscope manifest. Once you are aware of how your chart operates on an instinctual level, you can then work consciously with it to remove any obstacles to your growth.

The technique offered in this book is based upon the incorporation of the esoteric rulers of the signs and the integration of their polar opposites. This technique has been very successful in helping the client or reader modify existing negative energies in a horoscope so as to improve the quality of his or her life and the understanding of his or her psyche.

There is special focus in this huge comprehensive volume on the myths for each sign. Some signs may have as many as four different myths coming from all parts of the world. All are discussed by the author. There is also emphasis on the Jungian Archetypes involved with each sign.

This book has a depth often surprising to the readers of popular astrology books. It has a clarity of expression seldom found in books of the esoteric tradition. It is very easy to understand, even if you know nothing of Jungian philosophy or of mythology. It is intriguing, exciting and very helpful for all levels of astrologers.

0-87542-088-5
576 pp., 6 x 9, illus. $16.00

To order, call 1-800-THE MOON
Prices subject to change without notice

Animal-Speak
The Spiritual & Magical Powers of Creatures Great & Small

TED ANDREWS

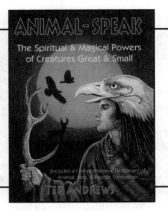

The animal world has much to teach us. Some are experts at survival and adaptation, some never get cancer, some embody strength and courage, while others exude playfulness. Animals remind us of the potential we can unfold, but before we can learn from them, we must first be able to speak with them.

In this book, myth and fact are combined in a manner that will teach you how to speak and understand the language of the animals in your life. *Animal-Speak* helps you meet and work with animals as totems and spirits—by learning the language of their behaviors within the physical world. It provides techniques for reading signs and omens in nature so you can open to higher perceptions and even prophecy. It reveals the hidden, mythical, and realistic roles of 45 animals, 60 birds, 8 insects, and 6 reptiles.

Animals will become a part of you, revealing to you the majesty and divine in all life. They will restore your childlike wonder of the world and strengthen your belief in magic, dreams, and possibilities.

0-87542-028-1
400 pp., 7 x 10, illus., photos $19.95

To order, call 1-800-THE MOON
Prices subject to change without notice

Dreams: Working Interactive
Registration Form

Llewellyn and the authors welcome your feedback about the *Dreams: Working Interactive* book and program. We encourage you to send your dreams and new symbol definitions to Stephanie Clement. She will personally respond to questions about your dreams, and your symbol questions and definitions will be considered for inclusion in updates to the program database.

Please take a few minutes to send us your name, address, and email address so that we can provide you with information about program and database updates.

Please print

Name _____

Mailing Address _____

City, State, Zip _____

Email Address_____

Phone (optional)_____

Please complete and mail this form to: Llewellyn Worldwide, Ltd., P.O. Box 64383, Dept. K145-7, St. Paul, MN 55164. Or if you prefer, email the information to dreams@llewellyn.com and mention *Dreams: Working Interactive*.
